TACTICS IN WOMEN'S SINGLES, DOUBLES, AND MIXED DOUBLES

TACTICS in Women's Singles, Doubles, and Mixed Doubles

By REX LARDNER

ILLUSTRATIONS BY GEORGE JANES

UNITED STATES LAWN TENNIS ASSOCIATION
TENNIS INSTRUCTIONAL SERIES

DOUBLEDAY & COMPANY, INC.
GARDEN CITY, NEW YORK
1975

ISBN: 0-385-090447 Trade
0-385-06733-X Paperbound
Library of Congress Catalog Card Number 74–12731
Copyright © 1975 by Rex Lardner
All Rights Reserved
Printed in the United States of America
First Edition

Contents

Introduction

More than nine million women play tennis in the United States. For the competitive woman player who wants to improve her game, tennis demands speed, the production of various kinds of strokes and spins, excellent reflexes, a sense of anticipation, coolness in an emergency, courage, sportsmanship, and the ability to gauge an opponent's weaknesses.

This is a book on the tactics that have been found the most effective for women in singles, doubles, and mixed doubles.

Tactics in tennis may be defined as the most efficient way to make use of one's best strokes to maneuver the opponent out of position and present her with a difficult or unreturnable shot.

Because singles is the quickest way to develop strokes, and tactics are relatively uncomplicated compared to the doubles game, the first section will cover singles. The second will take up doubles, and the third will deal with tactics in that charming game, mixed doubles.

TACTICS IN WOMEN'S SINGLES, DOUBLES, AND MIXED DOUBLES

I

. . . *But It Makes Demands*

Two vital elements of tennis must be stressed at the out-set: Your condition and your ability to place your shots where you wish in the enemy court. The first requires either that you play a great deal of tennis or do regular off-the-court exercises; the second, that you conscientiously practice all, or most, of the shots in the tennis arsenal—with a partner or, failing that, against a backboard. Knowledge of tactics is useless unless you can apply it.

Tennis, particularly singles, is an arduous game. To play it well, one should be in good physical condition. Stroking the ball, covering the court, running to the net, chasing down lobs, making difficult retrieves—all use up a great deal of energy. Your game suffers when you are tired. Concentration is difficult. Muscles tighten, tension sets in, and accuracy suffers. The determination to win falters. Orange juice can help, but only temporarily.

The following exercises are designed to strengthen the muscles the tennis player uses most: stomach, legs, hands, wrists and arms, shoulders and back. Ideally, you should perform these exercises on days you cannot be on a tennis court.

Endurance—the ability to summon one's resources to play well at the end of a tough match—is the most important physical asset of the tennis player, and must be given first consideration.

Running is the best way to build stamina. If you jog, fine. Jogging should be done every day that you are unable to play tennis, weather permitting. You should also try wind sprints: Run from twenty to thirty yards as fast as possible, rest for about thirty seconds and run back again. This builds both endurance and speed, and strengthens the legs. The first few times you might try four—at not quite top speed. As the days pass, you should work up to eight sprints. After achieving this goal, you can increase the length of the sprints and reduce the interval of rest between them. Your opponents will soon be surprised by your ability to cover the court—and play as well in the third set as in the first.

Skipping rope on days when running is impossible is splendid exercise for the tennis player, since this strengthens your arms as well as improves your footwork. Tennis requires a lot of side-stepping at the baseline, mainly to get into position without losing a step. While taking a walk you should turn sideways and do side steps for about ten yards, then face the other way and do them for ten more. You will find this quite tiring, but no prize was ever won without effort.

In the course of play, you do a good deal of bending and twisting, and stomach muscles are a main source of power in serving, smashing, and hitting hard ground strokes. These muscles should be given regular workouts when you are off the court. The number of such exercises is legion, but here are four that have proven useful:

Leg Lifts

Lie on your back, arms at sides, legs extended. Raise your legs about a foot and lower them. The number you start out with may be low at first—say, five—but it should be increased every day.

Flutter kick

From the same position, raise your feet two feet off the floor and flutter kick, legs approximately straight, for a count of twenty-five. Later the number can be increased.

Sit-ups

With the feet placed under something stable (a bookrack, for instance, or with ankles held by a partner), lie supine with the hands behind the head. Rise to a sitting position, then bend the head forward, touching the slightly bent knees with the elbows, and then returning to the supine position. Do this ten times. The exercise will stengthen the upper back, stomach, and thigh muscles. A variation is touching the left knee with the right elbow and the right knee with the left elbow alternately.

Woodchopper

Hold the hands overhead, fingers loosely locked, feet apart. Bend over and touch both hands to one foot. Then straighten up to the original position and bend over to touch the other foot. This is a splendid exercise for stomach, sides of the body, and thigh muscles.

Here are some leg and thigh exercises to supplement your jogging:

Knee Bends

Place hands on hips and with feet shoulder-width apart

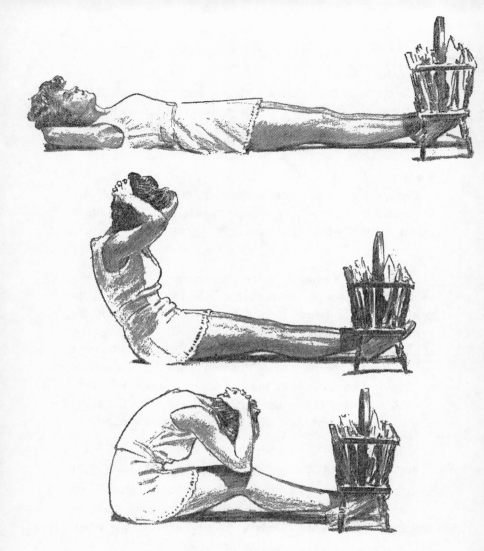

Sit-ups: With the feet placed under something stable (a book-rack, or your partner's hands), lie supine with the hands behind the head. Rise to a sitting position, then bend the head forward, touching the slightly bent knees with the elbows and returning to the supine position. Do this ten times. The exercise will strengthen the upper back, the stomach, and thigh muscles. A variation is touching the left knee with the right elbow and the right knee with the left elbow alternately.

Knee Bends: Stand with hands on hips, feet a few inches apart, and lower the body by bending the knees, weight balanced on the toes. The back should be kept nearly straight. Do this ten times. The exercise will improve balance and strengthen the thighs and calves. If the exercise is too difficult at first, the body can be lowered halfway down and raised again.

bend your knees to lower your body toward the floor—not all the way down, however. Hold for a second and rise to a standing position. The slower this exercise is done, the more effective it is. About five of these movements should be done originally, the number increasing with each session. If it is more comfortable, place a book, or two books, under your heels.

Alternating Single Knee Bend

Stand with your feet spread about twenty-four to twenty-eight inches apart, toes slightly out, hands on hips. By bending your right knee, move your torso to the right, keeping the body erect. Keep the left leg straight while placing weight on the right leg and thigh. After resuming the original standing position, repeat on the left side. Do about five for a start, then increase the number.

Toe Rises

Stand on the edge of a stair step, weight supported on the toes and balls of the feet, heels hanging over the edge. With one hand grasping the banister for balance, rise high on your toes, then lower the heels as far as possible. Hold each movement for about a second. Later on, toe rises can be done on one foot at a time. You should start with about ten and work on up.

With your feet similarly placed, place your hands on a step about four higher than the one your feet are on (as is comfortable). Move your knees forward alternately, as though running.

Wrist, Finger, and Forearm Exercises

Squeezing a rubber ball exercises the fingers, the wrist and forearm; it is assiduously practiced by many tourna-

Side Knee Bend: Stand with hands on hips, feet about twenty-four to twenty-eight inches apart, toes out. With the back erect, bend the left knee, shifting the body weight to the left. After going as low as is comfortable, rise to the original position. Alternate to the right. (A variation is to bounce on the left side, from three to five times, before alternating to the right.) Repeat each side knee bend ten times. The exercise is useful to strengthen thigh, calf, and ankle muscles and improve balance.

ment players. Strengthening of these parts of the body will improve your ability to control every stroke. Some athletes count the number of squeezes; others do it till their hands get tired.

Here is an isometric exercise (non-movement muscle resistance) useful for strengthening the fingers: Place your hands together, palms inward, fingers outspread, fingertips touching. Bend your elbows so that your hands are about eight inches in front of your chest. Press the fingertips of your right hand hard against those of your left hand and hold for a count of ten. Relax for a second, then repeat the exercise twice more. Then make fast grasping motions with the fingers—about fifty.

Back and Arm Exercises

Facing a table, the back of an easy chair, or some stationary object, support the weight of your body by keeping your hands spread apart and arms straight. With the body rigid, lower yourself as far as possible, then push yourself back up. This modified push-up should be done ten times at the start, the number gradually increased. The push-up can be done on the floor, with the weight partly supported by the knees.

Rotate your arms in the manner of a swimmer doing the crawl—about twenty-five times at first; then rotate them in the manner of a swimmer doing the backstroke—about twenty-five.

Take your racket and go through the serving motion and continue the follow through until the racket is in the starting position and serve again—a kind of circular movement. Do this twenty-five times at the start.

Semi Push-ups: With the weight supported by the knees and the extended arms and hands, lower the torso nearly to the floor and raise it to the starting position. Repeat ten times. The exercise will strengthen the arms, shoulders, and upper back.

Exercises While Walking

Walking is splendid exercise. It tones up the body, helps the blood circulate. It can also condition you for tennis.

Take very long steps—say twenty—and see if you do not feel it in your hamstrings. Walk extremely fast for about fifty paces—and see if you are not a little bit winded. Turn sideways and do side steps as fast as you can—about ten. Then turn the other way and do ten more. This exercise will help you when you need to cover the baseline during long rallies. You should also try to run backwards about fifteen steps. This is useful for backing up for lobs.

If you do not have time to do all the exercises, try to do half of them every day you don't jog. It is recommended that you consider objectively where your chief weaknesses are, as far as condition is concerned, and concentrate on correcting them. It is a good idea to keep a record of a particular exercise done so that you can check on your rate of improvement.

If possible, join a gym or health club in the winter, where a multiplicity of exercise equipment is available and you have company in your efforts to keep in tiptop shape. Organized indoor sports—badminton, swimming, skating, volleyball—are useful substitutes for the specialized exercises.

The important thing is to exercise *regularly*.

II

Tactics for All Seasons

When you are in good condition, your best strokes refined, your weaknesses diminishing, how do you make the best use of your skills to defeat a worthy opponent?

Tactics are concerned with a great number of variables: The special abilities of one's opponent, her aggressiveness or lack of it, her speed afoot, whether or not she is left-handed; the court surface, the wind and sun, the temperature; and many others.

Before attacking these individual problems it might be useful to set down some general stroking precepts that have been found to contain great wisdom. They are:

1. Keep your eye on the ball. If you miss a shot it is likely that this oversight was to blame. You should watch the flight of the ball as it comes off your opponent's racket and sails into your court. *Without allowing anything to distract you,* you should watch it as your racket sweeps through—but you should not jerk up your head to see its flight. As in golf, the head must be fixed in place when you hit and follow through. After the stroke is completed, pick up the flight of the ball again.

2. The moment the ball leaves your opponent's racket, move into position to return the shot, taking your racket back so you will not have to hurry the stroke.

3. The farther in front of the body the ball is met,

the more pace that can be applied. Generally speaking, if the tactical situation permits, it is better to hit cross court off both sides than down the line.

Here are some sound tactical principles:

1. When serving—in doubles especially—try to get the first serve in, even if it means taking some speed off the ball. Second serves, since they *must* go in, are often timidly hit and shallow. An alert receiver, aware of this, can assume the offensive with her return—if she does not win the point outright. In doubles, the net player, confronted with a receiver moving toward her thinks of nothing but protecting her health—which is understandable but may cost a point and does not make for a close bond between partners.

2. Always make a special effort when receiving to try to return the serve. Theoretically, if the serve is sent back, no matter how weakly, the other side may make an error.

3. Try hard to win the first point, the first game, the first set. This puts pressure on the enemy to play catch-up—and if the next point or game is lost the pressure mounts.

4. Play to the score. When you are ahead 40–love or 40–15 you can take chances—hard, flat drives followed by a sortie to the net, a leaping poach to slap the ball away, a more daring return of serve than usual, a harder second serve than ordinary. Important points to win occur at 30–15, 40–30, and deuce. They mean that one side or the other takes a commanding lead (or wins the game) or manages to draw even. More concentration than usual should be applied at these critical stages.

5. If your opponent seems tired, do not let her win

easy points; keep the ball moving and make her travel around the court.

6. After a long rally, do not commiserate with yourself if you lost it or blithely congratulate yourself if you won it. Both players being physically and mentally weary, the next point will probably be a short one. If you are alert to your opportunities you can sometimes count on your opponent's careless error.

7. In an informal match against markedly inferior opponents, take something off the ball and hit mainly to the stronger of the two. These concessions make for more enjoyment for everybody.

III

Varieties of Strokes

You can improve your game by playing a great deal of tennis—most often against better players—but your progress will be three times as fast if you utilize some playing time to perfect your strongest shots and strengthen the weak ones; and perhaps try new ones.

There are twelve basic strokes in tennis and five subtle or special strokes. The basic ones are:

The Serve: The beginning shot, made by tossing up and hitting the ball from behind the baseline so that it lands in the diagonally opposite service box. It is sometimes hit with marked slice and sometimes nearly flat.

The Forehand Drive: A stroke made by taking the ball on the right side of the body after it bounces and swinging through it when it is approximately at waist height, directing it to some area in the opponent's court. The drive may be hit flat or carry top spin. A drive with top spin can sail several feet over the net (a safety factor) and still stay within the bounds of the opponent's court. Either the Eastern Forehand or the Continental grip is used. (See illustrations.)

The Forehand Chop: Hitting down on the ball after it bounces on the right side and imparting severe underspin. The racket is held in a Continental grip and the

In the slice serve, the right-handed player holds the racket in the right hand, with a backhand grip, fingers holding firmly but not tightly. The body, when serving to the deuce court, is at approximately an 80-degree angle to the net; when serving to the ad court, it is turned somewhat to the right. The left foot is close to the baseline. The ball is held easily in the fingers—not the palm—of the left hand and the weight is evenly balanced on both feet.

The ball is tossed straight upward by the left hand, reaching a height of one foot above the point of release, as the right hand takes the racket back behind the head. Many players drop the frame of the racket behind the back in what is known as the "back-scratching position" prior to bringing it up to meet the ball.

The grip should now be very firm and the eyes kept on the ball until the racket actually hits it. As the racket is brought forward to slice across the ball, imparting left-to-right spin, the weight is transferred to the left foot. The momentum of the forward-moving arm and shoulder as the left arm is lowered will bring the right side of the body forward.

In a single fluid motion, the right leg and foot are brought over the baseline to add power to the serve and maintain balance.

In the forehand ground stroke, the racket is brought back
early, in a sideward (as opposed to looping) motion. The body
and racket are both approximately perpendicular to the net.
The weight, just before starting the forward swing, is shifted
forward onto the left foot, the left knee is bent, and a firm
base is established. The racket is cocked slightly backward
by the wrist.

Eyes watching the ball, the player starts the forward swing, conscious that the basic ground stroke is a down-to-up motion.

After the ball has been struck, the player brings the racket forward and upward in a smooth follow through. Top spin is imparted not by the turning of the wrist but by the natural forward and upward motion of the racket.

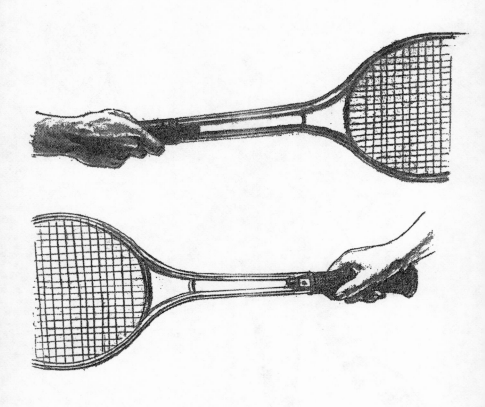

Eastern Forehand (*right and left views*): Here the player "shakes hands with the racket," the palm on the right side of the handle, where it can give good support. The forefinger is extended for better control of the racket head, while the thumb curls around the left side of the handle. The heel of the hand, for additional support and "feel," should rest against the butt of the racket. The palm of the hand, after the grip is assumed, lies in the same hitting plane as the racket.

Side view.

Side view.

Overhead view.

The Continental Forehand and Backhand Grips: These grips represent a cross between the Eastern Forehand and Eastern backhand. The V of the thumb and forefinger lies directly over the top of the handle, the grip remaining the same for hitting off both sides. The position of the hand gives the wrist more play (but less firmness) than the Eastern Forehand and back-hand, becoming a useful shot for chopping, slicing, and cutting the ball.

racket head is brought back to about shoulder height on the backswing. Then it is taken diagonally forward and down, meeting the ball at about hip height and about a foot in front of the body. The most famous female practitioner of the chop was Helen Jacobs, who won many championships (mainly on grass) with it. It is a useful shot to break up an opponent's rhythm, since the ball bounces more vertically than the conventional drive and the opponent must use extra speed to return it with depth. The reverse spin also tends to cause many returns to travel low, into the net. It is a useful counterstroke for high-bouncing drives with a great deal of top spin—and hit with very little effort. Some players hit a floating chop before moving to net, finding that the vertical bounce gives them more time to advance. It should not be considered a substitute for the drive, however (especially in doubles), because an experienced opponent can move in on it and hit a deep, forcing shot. Also, it often presents less of a problem for opposing net players than the conventional drive.

The Backhand Drive and Underspin Backhand: Two more basic strokes, accomplished by taking the ball on the left side after it bounces and directing it to some portion of the opponent's court. The drive is hit flat or (a much riskier shot) with top spin, using the Eastern backhand grip. Placing underspin on the backhand makes for better control of the shot, most women players find, and the bounce—low and nearly vertical—often bothers opponents. For underspin, the Continental grip is used.

The Forehand Volley: A ball hit crisply on the right side before it bounces, preferably with a downward motion.

In the backhand ground stroke, the position of the player after
the backswing is made is shown in two views. Note that the
racket has been taken back with the help of the left hand (fingers on the racket throat). This insures a complete body turn
before the racket is started forward. Just before the forward
motion is begun, the weight is transferred to the partly bent
right leg and a firm base is established. The elbow is partly
bent at the beginning of the forward motion of the right arm.

With the feet firmly based, the racket is brought forward and, with the right arm extended, the ball is struck in front of the right knee.

At the conclusion of the swing, the racket rises up in a smooth follow through, the left arm extended for balance.

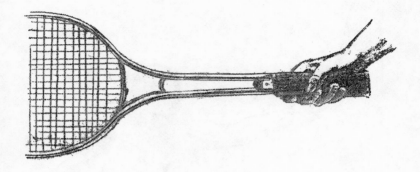

Eastern Backhand: In shifting over from the Eastern Forehand grip, the hand makes a one-eighth turn to the left so that the V between the thumb and forefinger is over the top left bevel of the handle, allowing the thumb to take its position almost diagonally across the left side of the handle. Again, the heel of the hand rests against the butt of the racket and the forefinger is extended for control.

Forehand Volley: Because the ball is hit before it bounces, it is harder to judge its speed and direction than it is for the forehand ground stroke. The player must concentrate hard, get the racket back early (using a relatively short backswing), grip the handle firmly, and try to keep the handle below the head. Note the placement of the player's weight on the forward foot and her partly turned body as the racket is brought forward to "punch" the ball into the opponent's court.

Most volleys are made from the forecourt; the closer to the net they are made, the more effective they are. Some players use the Eastern Forehand grip and some the Continental.

The Backhand Volley: Hitting the ball before it bounces on the left side. Since it is difficult to hit a backhand volley with the Eastern Forehand grip, the Eastern backhand should be used if there is time to change. Because this is often inconvenient, the Continental, which can be used off both sides, is recommended.

The Lob, Forehand and Backhand: A high, arching shot that passes over the head of an opponent at net or, ideally, drives a baseline opponent back by landing deep in her court. A *defensive* lob, with the racket held low and coming up under the ball, is hit especially high to allow the striker time, when out of position, to move into position in the center of the court. An *offensive* lob, with a lower trajectory, is hit when the opponent is close to the net, forcing her to retreat and chase down the ball. The striker should then move to the net.

The Overhead or Smash: An attacking shot generally hit from a point close to the net off a lob, a high volley, a high-bouncing drive, or a scooped-up retrieve. It is similar in motion to the serve and, in the case of replying to a lob, can be struck before the ball bounces or after. It may be hit flat—for speed—or with slice—for control and a skidding bounce.

The Backhand and Forehand Drop Shot: A delicately hit stroke, made with a brief chopping motion, that takes speed off the opponent's ball and, hit with underspin, makes a near-vertical bounce that forces her to run for-

Backhand Volley: This shot is probably the most difficult of all strokes for women. The player slips the thumb around behind the racket for greater support and turns the body at a more pronounced angle than for the forehand volley. Again the forward knee is bent, to allow the racket handle to lower for greater control of the ball.

In the smash or overhead the movements by the player are very much like those of the serve. As soon as it is evident that a lob has been struck, the player draws the racket behind her head and places herself in the proper position to hit the ball in front of her (at a spot about four feet over her head) as it descends. The weight is distributed evenly on both feet. Pointing with the finger of the left hand at the descending ball helps gauge the distance and the speed of the descent; it is also an aid to balance.

At the precise moment that the ball is at a height where the player can hit it with a fully extended arm, the racket is quickly brought forward in a service motion, the weight is transferred to the left foot and the left arm lowers as the left shoulder is turned to the left.

After the ball has been struck, the racket is brought down in a smooth follow through, the weight carried almost entirely on the forward foot.

ward and hit up. The recommended grip is the Continental for both forehand and backhand. If not used too frequently, it is a devastating return of serve.

The Half Volley: Generally hit from the forecourt, it consists of taking the ball immediately after it bounces from a position close to the forward foot. Since the ball is close to the ground when hit, the knees should be bent for control. Tightly gripping the racket, the striker uses little backswing and no follow through. Ideally, the ball should just skim the net. It is a difficult shot and one to be avoided except by experts. Better tactics are to move forward and hit the ball on the volley or move back and take it higher on the bounce.

The Lob Volley: Generally hit from the forecourt, this difficult shot is occasionally used to foil an opponent who is hugging the net and ready to pounce on any low shot. Player A tilts the face of her racket and swings under the ball so that it sails over the head of Player B. (If the lob is too low, Player A should face in the opposite direction for safety's sake.)

The Stop Volley: A touch shot by the net player. Instead of punching the ball sharply to an open area, she merely places her racket in the way of the ball and, with wrist and fingers slightly relaxed rather than firm, dumps it over the net. It is used when the opposite side is back, expecting a deep volley. Sometimes underspin is imparted to the ball, causing it to bounce nearly vertically.

The Backhand Smash: An offensive shot struck near the net. It is made by taking the racket over the left shoulder, the right arm bent into an L, the elbow raised to about nose height. The racket is brought back to meet a high lob on the left side, the body turning to the left. Then the upper arm is brought forward rapidly, straightening with a kind of snapping motion as the body wheels to the right. The ball is hit at a point about two feet in front of the body and about four feet higher than the head. It is a most difficult shot, used mainly to return the ball and not for tactical placement.

The Dink: A short cross-court return of a hard serve, made by blocking rather than stroking the ball, to remove some of its speed. It is directed at the feet of an inrushing server, forcing her (or him, in mixed) to hit a difficult volley or half volley, and allowing the receiver or, in doubles, the receiving team to hit down on the ball and take the offensive.

IV

Practice for Singles

The essential strokes in singles are: The serve, the forehand, the backhand, the lob, the drop shot, and the smash. Although it is not essential to volley well in singles, the serious player will find the stroke one of the most powerful tactical weapons in her repertoire. In the days of May Sutton Bundy, advancing to the net was considered eccentric, but today women are discovering that commanding the net may mean the difference between triumph and defeat. (In doubles, of course, the game is won or lost at the net and a sure volleying touch is essential.)

Before starting a series of practice sessions it is useful to know where one's weaknesses lie. For physiological reasons, women players are strong in some areas and less strong in others. The most powerful and dependable stroke for the woman player is generally her forehand drive. Her serve, usually not a blockbuster, is usually hit deep and is well aimed. Women as a rule lob well off the forehand and many have a sound forehand volley. However, women tend to lack confidence in the following strokes: The backhand ground stroke, the backhand volley, and the smash. The drop shot, a most useful tactical weapon in singles, is not often used.

Other characteristics of women's play are: Running

from side to side effortlessly, but experiencing difficulty in making a forward dash to the net—either to retrieve a drop shot or to take advantage of a weak return; having difficulty in judging shots hit with a great deal of spin, especially underspin and sidespin; and, at net, being content merely to *return* a volley rather than angle it deep for a point.

You should make special effort to improve these shots by frequent practice with a practice partner. If none is available, in most cases, practice against a wall is recommended.

THE SERVE

Take a bag of a dozen balls to an empty court and try hitting all of them to the forehand in the deuce court; to the backhand in the ad court; to the backhand in the deuce court; to the forehand in the ad court. Try to place your serves within two feet of the rear service line. Practice both slice and flat serves. Note the position of your feet and how it affects not only the direction of your serve, but also the height at which you toss the ball and the way the toss affects the depth and speed of the serve. Do not overdo serving practice the first few times, however, as your arm or shoulder may get sore.

If you are not getting power in your serve, ignore the service box and try to hit the opposite fence. Hitting this increased distance will strengthen arm and shoulder muscles and force you to place your weight behind the serve. Serving practice is also splendid practice for the overhead.

Practicing with a partner is always more fun than practicing alone. If you can, locate a player equally interested in improving her strokes and serve a dozen balls to her. She can practice serve returns. Then reverse the exercise.

If no courts are available, practice your serve against a backboard. Stand thirty-nine feet from the board and aim serves about two feet above a line representing the net. You can also practice other strokes against a backboard, such as the forehand drive and chop, the backhand drive and chop, the lob, the drop shot, and the smash. You can practice the half volley by standing about eight steps from the board and directing shots just over the net. Warning: On drives, the ball should not be hit hard because it comes back more quickly than one hit with a partner across the net and you may tend to hurry your swing. Strokes should be made smoothly and with great care. Moving in closer to the backboard, you can hit successive volleys with your forehand, then with your backhand. You can alternate lobs with smashes, as well as practice the latter about five yards from the backboard, with both your forehand and backhand. Since, in using a backboard, most ground strokes will be directed down the line, it is a good idea to hit cross court occasionally even if the ball is not retrievable. Emphasize your backhand shots, as these are usually the weakest on the courts.

With a partner, ground strokes can be practiced as follows: Exchange down-the-line forehands replied to by down-the-line backhands for five minutes, each player trying to keep the ball deep. Then exchange cross-court forehands for another five minutes. Follow with an exchange of cross-court backhands for eight minutes. Then hit down-the-line backhands returned by down-the-line forehands.

To practice the volley, stand at net while your partner hits balls within reach so that you can volley them back. Continue this for five minutes and then reverse positions. Once players have become proficient, the player at the baseline can try to pass the net player while the latter tries to make a placement.

A method of acquiring co-ordination and touch is for both players to stand at the juncture of the center service line and the rear service lines in each court and volley back and forth, keeping the ball low, making the partner hit up. It is essential to watch the ball and hold the racket firmly.

Lobs can be practiced in conjunction with smashes. One player smashes from the net, or near it, while the other replies with high lobs. When proficiency is gained, the player in the back of the court can send either a lob up or try to hit a drive past the net player, making the latter maneuver quickly to hit the proper return. If a player is particularly weak in one department, she should devote extra time to it and, with her playing partner's help, analyze what she might be doing wrong.

For drop-shot practice, the players stand about four yards from the net, diagonally opposite, and exchange drop shot forehands, then drop shot backhands. More serious practice consists of one player serving and the receiver drop-shotting diagonally, the server charging up to retrieve the ball and the receiver trying to score a point off the return. A down-the-line return of a drop shot is recommended.

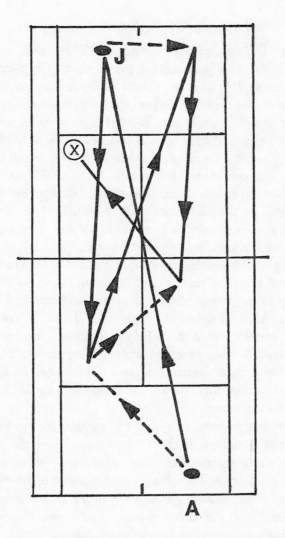

Approach Shot Drill: In this very useful exercise, Player A sends over a courtesy shot to J, who deliberately hits short. Player A advances on the ball and drives hard to J's backhand, moving to net to cut off J's attempted passing shot. Failing to take advantage of the opponent's short shots—those bouncing in the vicinity of the rear service lines—is a pronounced weakness in many players and is a skill that should be practiced assiduously.

Once the ground strokes and volley are confidently hit, the players can practice approach shots—deep drives to the corners, followed by a dash to the net and a volley or smash of the return. Player A sends the ball over and Player B deliberately hits short. Player A then moves in and hits the ball to a corner and comes to net. Player B tries a passing shot or lob and Player A tries to put the ball away. This continues for five minutes, then Player B practices her approach shots. The drop shot can likewise be practiced on the deliberately short-hit ball.

The return of service is an essential stroke in both singles and doubles, and should be given special attention. In singles, Player B serves to Player A's backhand and Player A aims the return deep to various areas of B's court —deep to the forehand and deep to the backhand, for instance. After the forehand and backhand returns have been practiced for a time, Player B can mix up her serves as Player A tries to make aggressive returns. This drill helps develop concentration and confidence. In doubles, ground strokes, lobs, dinks, and drop shots should be practiced on the return.

Constant practice can be fairly tedious for persons of a competitive nature. If this is the case, players should play practice sets against each other at the end of the practice session. On other occasions, serious sets can be played— not to forget serious sets against other rivals to see how beneficial the practice sessions have been. You will be pleasantly surprised at your new conquests.

V

Singles Tactics

Singles is that most primitive of challenges—head-to-head combat against a determined opponent, with no one to help and no substitutions. Even between players familiar with one another's styles and skills, there is a feeling-out process at the beginning of a match, since an opponent can be on or off, may have improved a weakness, or may have changed her game tactically. A little later on in the match, one player may show more fatigue than the other. Additional variables include the weather and the court surface. Some players are more effective indoors than out. Susceptibility to having one's concentration broken and refusal to let one's concentration be broken often determine the outcome of a match.

During the warm-up and the first few games, the general situation should be probed. The effectiveness of one's own strokes under these particular conditions should be gauged. Whatever weaknesses are uncovered in the opponent—slowness afoot, weak overhead, weak backhand, and so on—should be attacked; one's own weaknesses should be protected or hidden as much as possible. Knowledge should accumulate as the match progresses and new tactics should be devised. In most tennis, the victor is not the player with the more classic strokes but the player who uses her strokes more effectively.

THE SERVE

The server puts the ball in play from a stationary position, from a spot she chooses behind the baseline and aims the ball into the service box diagonally opposite. Ideally, she directs the course of action and, if her serve is dependable and she can capitalize on the receiver's return, she should win the game.

Consider the possibilities: The server can win the point outright with a well-directed delivery. She can force the opponent to hit a weak return (one that lands close to the service line) which the server can hit deep, move behind the shot, and lay siege at the net. She can pull her opponent out of the court with a wide serve and then make her run to the opposite side to retrieve a shot to the opposite corner. By varying the direction, speed, and spin of her serve she can keep the receiver off-balance, psychologically dominating the course of play.

The best aim points for a server serving to the deuce court are: Deep to the forehand, deep to the backhand, and very wide to the forehand. In serving to the ad court, the best aim points are: Deep to the backhand, sharply angled to the backhand, and wide to the forehand—down the middle. Occasionally a shot aimed directly at the receiver will cause confusion and probably result in a weak return. In the majority of cases the server should stand next to the center line when serving to the deuce court, protecting her backhand side as much as possible; and a yard from the left singles sideline when serving to the ad court. This position gives her a good angle for a deep serve to the backhand while reducing the amount of territory available for an attempted return to the server's backhand.

If the return is shallow, the server should attack it, driving to the opposite corner. If she has confidence in her approach shot and net game, she could come in behind it—always wary of a lob return. If the receiver is drawn far out of court, the server has three choices: She can hit a drive to the opposite corner; a drive to the corner the receiver has just left if she has been found slow in changing direction; or a drop shot that barely clears the net at the point farthest away from the opponent.

After her delivery, the server should be ready to move sidewise, diagonally, or quickly forward. Good reflexes are necessary to get a jump on the ball, especially when it is a return of the ordinarily weaker second serve. The opponent's patterns of returns should be noted. Does she like to hit cross court or down the line on her forehand? Does she seldom hit a down-the-line backhand from the ad court? Does she prefer a fast serve to one with spin? Does she blast away at the second serve, hoping to win the point outright? (If she is successful at this, you had better get the first serve in or put something extra on the second serve.) Does she often make drop-shot returns? From which court? Is she content merely to make a safe return? Does she consistently hit back your hardest serves? (If this is the case, you might as well save some energy for other elements of the game.)

These reactions should be filed away so that the server can adjust her tactics accordingly.

Serves should be varied as to speed, the amount of spin put on the ball, and the aim point. Sometimes a deliberately slow or shallow first serve will draw an error because of the surprise element. Sometimes the second serve should be hit hard; it may be good for an outright point against an opponent ready to stalk a feeble second serve. On certain points—15–30, 30–40, and ad out—the first serve *must* go in. If it does not, the game is virtually lost because the opponent is ready to do all sorts of wicked things to the timidly offered second serve.

VI

Receiving the Serve in Singles

It is essential to develop a steady return of serve. The return need not be a winner, but one should avoid giving the server an easy point. Even a severe, well-placed serve can be lobbed back or blocked or scrambled for and pushed back in some manner—if the receiver is alert and ready to move quickly. The server, faced with the return, must now put the ball away or hit an offensive shot—and she may miss for any number of reasons. Or she may hit a ball fairly easy to return, making the contest a matter of who is going to win the rally. The theory of "keeping the ball in play"—advocated by everyone from Tilden to Chris Evert—holds for this element of the game as well as for the others.

Many women do not consistently hit strong serves, and when the serve is vulnerable it should be attacked; the receiver can then take the offensive. Short serves, slow serves, high-bouncing serves—these deliveries can all be pounced on by the aggressive-minded receiver, causing trouble for the server. Not only will she probably lose the point, but her morale will suffer as well. She will be forced to serve harder—an exigency that will probably result in a string of double faults and further shattering of the morale.

Against a relatively weak server, the receiver should

consider on which side she wishes to take the ball and take her receiving position accordingly. If she prefers to take it on her backhand, she should move to the right and leave an opening there. This is a tacit challenge for the server to place the ball there and in most cases she will respond. If the receiver wishes to take the ball on her forehand, she should move to her left. Having stuck her neck out—for there is danger of an ace or near-ace on the forehand side if the server hits where she aims or gets lucky—she must carefully watch the toss and the motion of racket striking ball so that she can immediately gauge where the ball is headed and dart to that spot. If she has confidence in her backhand she need not play as far to the left.

In the deuce court the most effective forehand return against a right-hander is down the line—to the server's backhand—and deep within the bounds of safety. Care should be taken that the ball does not pass beyond the baseline or sideline; the aim point should be two or three feet from the juncture of these lines. The server, running to her left to return this difficult shot, may well hit the ball short. The receiver should then hit a drive to the forehand corner and take the net, ready to volley an attempted passing shot or smash a lob.

If the backhand return by the server is a lob, the receiver should move into position and, carefully watching the ball as it descends (and after it bounces), smash to one corner or the other, moving to net after the smash. For safety's sake the smash should be directed to the most open part of the court; it should not be hurried, and the smasher should remember that, statistically, more

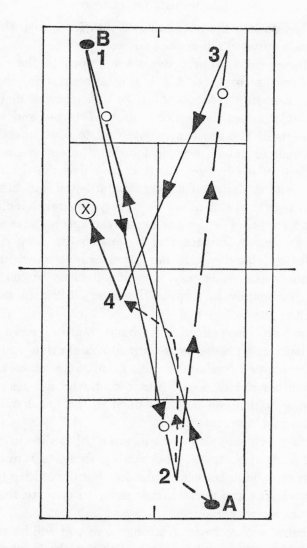

The Secret Advance: Player A hits deep to B's forehand, then takes the return and hits a high attacking lob (dashed lines) to B's backhand, darting to net as B chases down the ball. Unaware of A's move, B hits a relatively weak shot which A puts away for the point.

smashes go into the net than sail out. The stroke should be made outward rather than down.

The second most effective serve return in the deuce court on the forehand side is a cross-court drop shot—a stroke women players do not make sufficient use of. Properly hit, it forces the server to dash up to net and scoop up the ball. The receiver, moving up to cover a counter drop shot or handle a weak lob, has the entire court in which to place her return. It is true that the drop-shot artist is often hoist on her own petard—the ball hits the net or goes too deep, allowing the server to polish it off.

The drop-shot return has two advantages: It makes the receiver hustle forward and it sets up the deep down-the-line forehand return; the server cannot travel in two directions simultaneously. The effectiveness of the drop shot lies mainly in surprise, however; it should not be used too often.

The third most effective forehand return of serve from the deuce court is the cross-court forehand drive—hit deep to the server's forehand corner or hit at a sharp angle, pulling her out of court. Either shot may draw a weak response which can be rifled deep to the backhand corner for an almost sure point.

Other forehand serve returns are a sharp slice to either side, a high lob to the backhand—difficult to return because of its high bounce—and a soft but deep drive to the center of the court which may draw an error because of its unexpectedness.

Against a player with a strong serve you will be taking many shots on your backhand. If this stroke is weak, try to hit the return to the server's backhand by blocking or lobbing the ball. If you have confidence on this side, drive the ball to the server's backhand or slice it to her forehand. A very effective return, because it is unexpected, is a cross-court drop shot, hit with considerable underspin. If it is executed properly it is a sure point for the receiver.

In the ad court, because of the long diagonal into which the server can angle the ball, you should play quite far to the left to avoid taking the ball on your backhand. (Aces to the forehand side in this court are much more difficult to hit than in the deuce court.)

The most effective return is a deep cross-court forehand to the server's backhand. A strong return will pull the server out of court and open up her forehand side for a placement. The second most effective return is a forehand to the server's forehand corner—a drive or a chop—making her race to reach the ball, leaving her backhand corner exposed. A deep lob to the backhand and the cross-court drop may also present difficulties.

One reason for developing a dependable backhand is the use to which it can be put when you receive in the ad court. The down-the-line shot is more comfortable from the backhand side, as is the deep cross court, and the cross-court drop can be devastating. If your backhand is strong, you can tempt the server to hit there by leaving extra room on that side. Expecting the serve there, you can hit shots in all directions, at various heights and speeds and angles—most of which are directed to her backhand, giving you the choice of pounding it until she misses or slapping the ball to the opening on her forehand side.

If your own serve is not particularly strong, you should make a special effort to break through your opponent's. If you fail to do this a couple of times you may lose the set.

VII

Winning Rallies

In women's singles the server does not win the greater proportion of games (as in men's tennis); nor are points quickly decided by a well-placed volley, a smash, or crisply hit passing shot. Women's strokes are characterized more by finesse and guile than bullet speed, and rallies are usually longer. The opportunity for tactics is therefore greater. (Women's tennis, for those reasons, is more interesting to watch than men's, as Billie Jean King contends.)

Apart from the opponent's making a careless error—like blowing a setup—there are four ways to win rallies: By working your opponent out of position and hitting a shot that captures the point outright or forces a weak return that can be attacked for the point; discovering a pronounced weakness that can be taken advantage of until an error results; outsteadying her in a war of attrition; and putting pressure on her, forcing an error.

FORCING A WEAK RETURN

This is done by keeping your ground strokes deep and making your opponent run from one side of the court to the other; it is much more difficult to hit a shot while racing toward it than drifting easily into position. If you can hit close to the sidelines without too much risk, mix up drives with chops and, always ready to move forward, take advantage of any short ball your opponent sends back. Moving up, you can sharply angle her return to an open part of the court. If your opponent retrieves it, she will be out of position to handle a drive to the opposite corner or a drop shot.

ATTACKING WEAKNESSES

Weaknesses exist in every player. They may be a particular stroke, too much reliance on a particular stroke, impatience, or inability to cover the court. If the flawed stroke is the opponent's backhand, a shot should be directed far to the forehand side, after which a shot should be sent wide to the backhand. (It is sometimes more feasible to attack weakness through strength. This stratagem is especially useful if your opponent plays far to her left to protect her backhand.) Often a series of shots to an opponent's weakness—pounding it—will result in an error. Switching unexpectedly for a moment to her strength may also draw an error.

It may be that your opponent has trouble on one side or the other in returning spin. If so, again a shot should be directed to her strong side, after which decided spin is imparted to a ball hit to her weaker side. If confident of your volley, you should move up.

If, when you play net, she very seldom lobs, you can play closer than usual, making the volley easier. If she

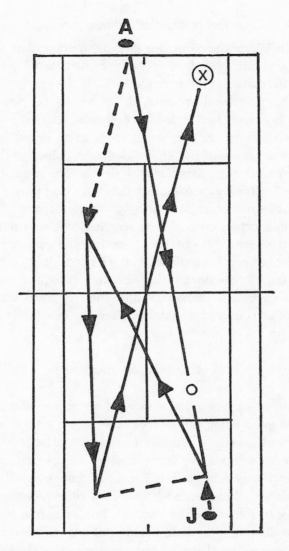

Drop-Shot Return of Serve: Player A has hit a shallow second serve to J, who moves forward and hits an underspin cross-court drop shot. Player A must rush forward to scoop it up, whereupon J drives her weak return to the far corner. If A's return is too fast to drive accurately, J can lob to this area. She should then position herself at the net to cut off a possible drive or smash a possible lob.

has little confidence in her passing shots and invariably lobs, you can play farther away from the net and drift back to smash her lob returns.

If her overhead is weak, draw her to net with drop shots and feed her high lobs (especially when she faces the sun). If her serve is weak, move in on it and take the offensive immediately. If she does not volley well, bring her forward, then pass her with drives. The drop shot is a very effective weapon against a slow-moving player or one with slow reactions. It is tiring to chase forward after the ball, and often, even if it is reached, the return will be missed or weakly sent back, leaving the opponent's entire court open for a placement. The combination of drop shot and lob is a devastating one that forces the opponent to rush forward then back and then forward again. In the latter stages of a match especially, this tactic is very effective.

OUTSTEADYING AN OPPONENT

If your opponent is a dogged retriever who seldom misses even when off-balance, the surest way to disconcert her is to apply pressure (see next section). A second method of breaking up her game is to widely vary the kind of shot you give her to hit. You must change speed, height and depth, direction and spin so that she never has a chance to return the same sort of shot twice in a row. This means chopping the ball, blooping it over the net, sending over conventional drives to move her around the court, and drop-shotting to draw her forward.

Should she take the net, vary passing shots with lobs

—the latter probably being the more effective. It is difficult to smash into the opponent's court more than four times in a row, and the wear and tear on her arm and nerves may make her winning of the point a Pyrrhic victory. You must be ready to move in and attack a short ball, since this will give her less time to get into position for her return.

The danger in competing with this type of player is that, through trying too hard to put a ball beyond her reach, you hit too long or too wide. It is a situation she relishes, even as the aggressive player delights in making an unreturnable volley. You must be very careful to work her out of position before hitting a shot that is likely to force an error. Players of this type are in excellent condition and rely on the internal mental battle of the opponent to win points for them. The very top players, having a bad day or playing on surfaces that lend themselves to a retrieving type of game, have gone to pieces after a series of endless rallies. Lea Pericoli of Italy on a clay court is a master of retrieving play, can lob forever, and has beaten the world's best players.

On the other hand, since the retriever is a nonaggressive player, your ground strokes can clear the net by a safe margin and if you anticipate well you need not chase hard after her returns. Trying to defeat a very steady player by merely getting the ball back can wear down one's patience and eventually cause a psychological explosion: Your game will have been broken.

The moral is that you should develop a wide variety of strokes through practice with a playing partner and experiment with them during friendly matches. The most effective tactic is drawing the retriever close to the net and then lobbing—thus the drop shot and lob should be practiced assiduously.

PUTTING PRESSURE ON THE OPPONENT

This is undoubtedly the surest and most satisfying way to win a rally—imposing your will, like a Clausewitz general, on the adversary, making her scramble to return the ball and then firing the setups offered to all parts of the court.

It is done by taking the net.

The main value of this maneuver is the pressure it generates. Your opponent may err because she hurries her shot, because she fears what you, standing comfortably in her purview and alert to her possible returns, will do with the ball. She may direct an attempted passing shot too low (into the net), too high (beyond the baseline), or too warily (past a sideline). Additionally she worries, when you are in the back of the court, about hitting a short shot that will propel you forward and netward. Thus many of her replies will soar over the baseline. If she relies on lobs when you are at net you can move back and place them (not necessarily hard) into corners of the court. Even if she successfully passes you a few times or you hit a smash or two out or in the net, the odds are with you from the standpoint of tactics and psychology. Playing this kind of game presupposes that, through practice and hard matches, you (1) hit sound approach shots, (2) do not mind running forward and occasionally scampering backward, (3) have firm confidence in your volley, and (4) are in tiptop shape.

Taking the net is also a useful tactic against the player who hits aggressively and herself moves forward at every opportunity. If she volleys away your best ground strokes and smashes your lobs out of reach, you have little recourse but to capture the top of the hill, as it were, before she does. It cannot contain both of you. It might be that, in developing her net game she has neglected her ground strokes. Even if you are slightly uncomfortable there, you are still better off than if you played an entirely defensive game.

VIII

Handling a Lefty

The majority of players a right-hander comes up against are right-handers. But about one in twenty (the percentage is one in eleven for males) will be left-handers—which presents nineteen out of twenty players with a problem.

You hit to what should be her weakness (the backhand), and this turns out to be her great source of strength—the forehand. When she is at net, you pump a lob over her left shoulder—a classic shot—and stare into the face of a hard smash. You see an opening when she is at net—on her backhand—and it turns out to be her forehand; she puts the ball away. Her serve is confusing. The sidespin takes the ball to your left after it bounces, not the right. In the ad court you are pulled wide and forced to take the ball on your backhand, opening up the right side of the court into which she can place your return.

Pitted against a left-hander you must recast your tactical thinking and forswear the usual aim points. Her weakest shots will stem from her right side, for the backhands of left-handers are no stronger and often weaker than those of your right-handed opponents. Therefore hit most of your backhands down the line and your forehands cross court. Lob over her right shoulder. When serving, send the ball wide to the lefty's backhand in the deuce court; you may be rewarded with a weak return.

Watch out for sharply angled serves to your forehand in the deuce court; in the ad court be ready for a serve to your backhand that will bounce away from you. Warning: The spin on this serve may tend to cause most of your returns to fly to your left; on down-the-line backhands, aim well inside the sideline or the ball will sail out. You must concentrate for the first few games on precisely where you are hitting every shot; then you will probably become adjusted to the situation.

To prepare for a match against a left-hander you can pretend that a right-handed opponent is weaker on her right side and direct most of your shots there. Or you can locate a left-handed player, male or female, to hit with, where the tune-up is more realistic. In actual combat, during the warm-up or contest with your left-handed opponent, note if she has weaknesses: Slowness in moving about the court, unwillingness to take the net, erratic strokes, a weak second serve. These elements can be attacked, just as they can in a right-hander.

ASIDE TO LEFT-HANDERS

At the risk of betraying my own kind, I suggest the following: With your natural advantage, you should practice and make special use of your strong points—forehand, smash, serve, and forehand volley—so that these become devastating forcing shots which keep your opponent off-balance and on the defensive. After a deep drive to the backhand you should take the net in menacing style and dominate the court. When time permits, you should assiduously practice whatever weaknesses you may have: Possibly backhand, backhand volley, backhand lob. And develop those strokes perhaps not yet perfected: The drop shot, half volley, and backhand smash. Then the only party you have to watch out for is another left-hander.

IX

Sure Cure for Ragged Play

Sometimes you find you cannot hit anything right. Your serve returns either sail out or are hit short, where your opponent lambastes them. You are making tactical errors, like trying to hit a drop shot from the back of the court that plops in the net, and your down-the-line shots all fall wide. You can't get the first serve in and the second is returned forcefully. Missing several shots at net, you don't dare venture forward when the opportunity arises. In addition, your aggressive opponent is getting all the breaks—shots that hit the lines, net cord shots, shots that take bad bounces.

Getting mad at yourself is the second worst thing you can do. Giving up is the worst. Your purpose is to restore confidence in yourself and your shots—a mental state that can be reached by physical means. Here are the keys:

1. You are making these errors and playing well below your capabilities because you have lost concentration. The effect is cyclical: The more errors you make, the more difficult it is to concentrate. Like a general who has suffered a disastrous defeat you must regroup and wait for the opportunity to launch an attack. Outside noises, the menace of the enemy, the breaks she is getting —these influences keep you from thinking about your main objective and shred whatever concentration you have

left. In this situation, forget about your opponent and focus your entire attention on the ball. Before a match Billie Jean King has been known to sit down and stare at a tennis ball for a half hour. Many top players, when picking up or holding a ball before serving, stare at it for a second or two. When you serve, carefully watch the ball as you toss it up and as your racket meets it. (Also toss the ball a little higher than you have been doing; tension makes us all toss the ball too low, hurrying the serve.) When your opponent returns a shot, watch the ball as it comes off her racket, prepare to meet it, and watch it closely as your racket sweeps through.

2. You may be playing badly because you are tired. Minor annoyances disturb the flow of concentration. Put them out of your mind. Move at a leisurely pace between points, take deep breaths before serving and receiving, let tension subside. Move slowly when changing courts. Towel off slowly. Anticipate your opponent's shots, try to get a jump on the ball as it leaves your opponent's racket. Just before you hit, grip the racket tight; tired players can restore a great deal of control by this simple correction.

3. Assume that every shot you hit is going to be hit back; do not allow yourself to be surprised by valiant returns.

4. For a while hit well inside the lines and make sure that you clear the net by a safe margin. Make your opponent earn her points. As your game is restored to normal you can make bolder shots.

5. Should you miss a shot, do not fret about it. Think about the next point.

Mainly, make a positive, determined effort to put score, opponent's surge, distractions, and bad breaks out of your mind and immerse yourself in the task at hand—hitting the ball consistently and effectively. You know you have played and can play several levels better. It is just a question of reaching those levels before time runs out.

X

Doubles—the Fencing Match

The game of doubles is much more intricate than singles. Played between two evenly matched teams it can be decidedly complex. Two players instead of one are trying to find open spaces in the court into which to place the ball and two other players are trying to close these gaps and create openings for their own placements. Two players must be outguessed instead of one. The server is abetted by a partner at net who is going to try to put away any return that comes near her. Though the court is wider by nine feet for rallying, twice as many occupants protect it and they do not have as far to run, in most cases, as the singles player. On the other hand, the posting of one or both players at the net puts an immense burden on the opponents. A singles player can often be relatively careless about some of her shots; a doubles player faced with an enemy at net must hit her drives harder, lower, and more accurately. Otherwise they are going to be cut off for a point. The punishment for a mental lapse in singles can often be mitigated by hard running, outguessing, or scrambling; in doubles the first tactical mistake or poorly hit shot usually ends the point.

In doubles one must place great reliance on her partner. One player sets up the shot and her partner kills the return. One player sees her partner cannot get to the ball so she sets about retrieving it. One player is run far out of court; her partner moves over to protect as much of the exposed space as she dares. One player makes a stab for a difficult shot and misses it entirely; her partner, backing her up, manages to lay her racket on it and save the point. One player dashes across the net to intercept a shot but the ball is directed to the spot that she has left; her partner, darting over, manages to send up a lob; one player hits a shot deep to an opponent's backhand; both players run up to the net to present a formidable barrier.

Doubles does not require the stamina demanded by singles—though it requires a great deal—but it does call for more court craft, with the element of teamwork added, which may partly explain its great popularity among women players.

Because of the factor of two against two, the almost constant presence of a player (on either side) at net during rallies, the aid the server derives from her partner stationed at net, the greater width of the court and a number of other factors, doubles employs a different set of tactics. The shots in doubles, as a result, differ to a great extent from those used in singles.

In singles, the down-the-line return of a deuce-court serve is the soundest shot in the book. It is wasted in doubles—except on those rare occasions when the receiver wishes to keep the net player honest. The same with the down-the-line return of a serve in the ad court. The net player will simply murder it. The drop shot is not so effective in doubles, because there are two players ready to retrieve it, and the player in backcourt should be alert to move forward anyway.

Retrieving ability, an essential talent for the singles player, is handy in doubles, but with two opponents ready to pounce on any weak return, its value can be overestimated. The lob is a much more valuable tool in doubles than in singles because it is a most useful way to dislodge one's opponents from the net. It also enables the lobbing team to take the net themselves. The complement of the lob—the smash—is also a most important tool in doubles. If a lob is short, the smasher may very well win the point outright; on the other hand, if a player's smash is weak, she will find herself looking at swarms of lobs and losing points by the handful.

The stroke made far more use of in doubles than in singles, however, is the volley. Properly played, doubles is a constant skirmish to see which team can gain and keep control of the net. The pair that moves continually forward and is difficult to dislodge is almost always the victor. Admittedly, dashing forward and sometimes retreating to chase down lobs takes a lot of energy, but the results are gratifying. A kill is more satisfying than winning the point through an opponent's error. And a crisply hit volley that sails between one's opponents and strikes the fence before they see it makes one want to celebrate. If two players at net face two opponents at the baseline, the former should win the majority of the points.

The damage that the net player, or net players, can do is the reason why the serving team wins most of its games. The receiver's choice of returns is limited by the presence of the net player who, if she is alert and determined, can cover nearly half the net area. During a rally, the server may join her and a nearly impenetrable barrier is set up (assuming that the team has reasonable confidence in its volleying ability). The lob is called for as a practical defensive maneuver—but if it is short it can be smashed —and smashed and smashed. If the lob sails out, that is gravy for the net players.

A good backhand drive is useful in doubles but nowhere near as valuable as a good net game. A steady forehand drive that keeps the ball away from the net player and keeps her partner back is extremely useful. A steady serve (not a particularly fast one) is essential; double-faulting in doubles shatters your partner's morale (unless she has this habit herself). A lob that goes deep and which can be hit under adverse circumstances is most handy. The drop shot—as a return of serve—is an extremely potent weapon, since it keeps the server guessing: Should she come in to scoop it up? Should she stay back, expecting a deep drive or lob return of serve? Pressure on the server makes the game interesting. The smash is essential—for its psychological effect as well as its scoring power.

Tactical maneuvers that should be practiced—in an informal match or against a weaker team—include: Moving quickly to net, in company with your partner, after a deep approach shot; dashing forward when a lob has driven one or both opponents from the net; poaching and fake-poaching; racing back diagonally so that a lob can be taken on the forehand rather than the backhand; retreating rapidly to the baseline to set up a defensive wall after your partner has sent up a short lob that is sure to be smashed; coming to net after an aggressive return of serve; darting behind your partner to return a lob that has passed over her head on the backhand side.

XI

The Serve in Doubles

It is vital for you, as server, to win your serve in doubles, since every loss means a swing of two games. What might have been two to two turns out to be three to one in favor of the opponents. Now their serve must be broken and your team's serve must be held to keep you in the set.

The responsibility for winning the serve rests very largely with the server and she must take care not to carelessly lose points. (If she is fortunate enough to be partnered with a skilled and psychic poacher her responsibility descends to about 60 per cent. Let us assume that the partner at net is of average ability, however.)

In serving to the deuce court, the best aim points are deep to the receiver's backhand, deep to the receiver's forehand and very wide to the receiver's forehand. (On the last two types of serve, the net player should hug her alley, as the opportunity is great for a forehand down-the-line shot past her backhand. Should she be alert for this shot when it comes, however, she can make an easy putaway.)

The usual return from this court is to the server's forehand. If the return is shallow, the server's reply should be directed cross court or down the middle, the server moving in to net. If it is deep it is unwise for the server to try to win the point outright. Her best return is a cross-court drive kept well away from the receiver's partner, who may be closing in at net. If the receiver's partner is close to the net, the server can lob over her head, moving up behind the shot once she is sure the net player cannot smash it. If the net player on the receiving team leaves her alley uncovered, an occasional shot down the line may be rewarding, but it is a lost point against an alert player.

A favorite return of some receivers in the deuce court is a lob over the net player's head. If she cannot reach it, the server must run to her left and take the ball on her backhand, the net player immediately moving laterally to her right to protect the open side of the court. If the lob is a shallow one, the net player on the receiving team retreats to the baseline to defend against a smash. Of the possible returns of the lob by the server, hitting a backhand drive cross court is risky because the receiver's partner may have posted herself at the net to take advantage of the open spaces in the serving team's court. And a down-the-line shot or shot to the middle may be picked off by one of the opponents. The safest reply is another lob directed cross court. If it is sufficiently deep, the server can come to net to join her partner and the team takes the offensive.

Serves to the ad court are most often directed deep to the receiver's backhand, while occasionally they are aimed for the receiver's forehand or hit fairly shallow and wide to the backhand for the purpose of drawing her out of court and opening up the middle. It is essential that about 75 per cent of first serves go in. A weak second serve allows the ad-court receiver to do a number of things with the ball: Drop-shot it, take the net after a deep drive, slam the ball at the net player or make a clean placement down the middle or cross court. Even though speed is taken off the first ball, the advantage rests with the serving team as long as the first ball goes in. Occasionally, to keep the receiving team off-balance, the second serve should be hit as hard as the first.

From the ad court the return is almost always to the server's backhand; occasionally it comes down the middle, past the net player's backhand. Sometimes wide serves to the receiver's backhand are directed down the alley—mainly to keep the server's partner from acting too lively at the net. Some receivers in the ad court like to hit drop shots cross court off both forehand and backhand, forcing the server to dash in and scoop the ball up on her backhand. The server should always consider this possible return and be ready to run forward. Her partner at net should be alert for this return, too, as sometimes, because of its lack of speed and low trajectory, the drop shot can be picked off in midair and slapped down the middle for a point.

XII

Return of the Serve in Doubles

From a statistical standpoint, return of serve is probably the most important shot in doubles. The server starts with an initial advantage: She aims the ball where she thinks it will do the most damage and she has a helper at net who restricts the number of possible returns of the receiver. But if the return is good, the serving team must win the point by stroking and tactics, just as the receiving team must. The odds then go down to about even.

It follows that the return of serve must land somewhere in the opponents' court, out of reach of the net player and not furnishing the server with the opportunity to make a forcing shot. The receiver should also bear in mind that if the serve is weak, her team can assume the offensive.

The receiver has several returns available on forehand and backhand in both the deuce and ad court—some more effective against certain opponents than others.

On a serve to the forehand in the deuce court, the receiver can hit a deep cross-court to the server's forehand; a drive down the middle (if the net player hugs her alley) to the server's backhand; a cross-court drop shot that makes the receiver run forward and hit up; a sharply angled chop that pulls the server out of court; and a lob over the net player's head that the server must take on her backhand. If the server is driven back, both members of the receiving team should come forward and take the net.

If the serve comes to the (presumably weaker) backhand, the deuce-court receiver can hit cross court as deep as possible within the bounds of safety, drop shot, lob to the server, or lob over the net player's head.

Should the server dash to net on her serve, the best return is a lob over the net player's head and the second best a low drive that lands at the incoming server's feet.

Occasional shots, particularly on weak serves, should be aimed down the net player's alley—to test her ability to volley and her alertness.

In the ad court the receiver can protect her backhand, if desired, by standing far to the left. She may be occasionally aced on the right and have difficulty with a serve deep in the corner of the service court, but most of the time she will be able to hit forehand returns. These should be directed deep cross court, to the server's backhand, or hit with sidespin and sharply angled, so that the server must run forward and take a low-bouncing shot on her backhand. She can also loft an occasional lob over the net player's head.

It is extremely handy, however, to have a good reliable backhand when receiving in this court. Backhand drives or chops can be sent cross court to the server's backhand; the backhand drop shot can be more severely angled than the forehand drop shot; the service box can be covered more readily (fewer chances of unreturnable serves and aces); the down-the-line shot on a wide serve is much more comfortably hit; and the lob return is more easily disguised from that side.

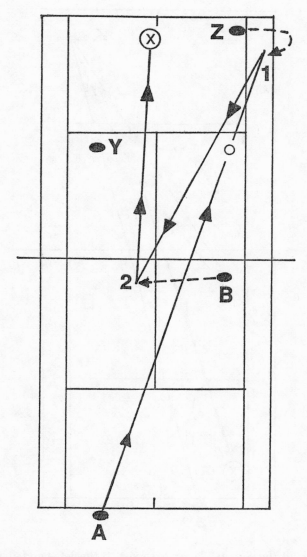

Running Around the Backhand: Here Server A has placed the ball in the backhand corner of Z's service box. Player Z moves to take it on her stronger forehand, however, putting herself out of position to retrieve B's volley as she poaches wide to her left and punches the ball down the middle.

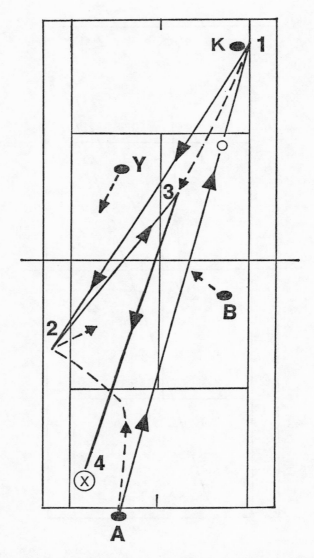

Attacking the Serve: Player A serves to the left-handed K in the ad court. Player K attacks the ball, hitting wide to A's backhand and following her shot to net. Partner Y moves forward with her to protect the alley. A hits to the center of the court and K volleys sharply between the serving team for a placement.

If the server runs in behind her delivery, the receiver lobs, or hits low and hard cross court, or sharply angles a soft ball that the server must take on her backhand.

Receivers in both courts should think offensively. If the service is weak (particularly the second) the receiver should move in a step and attack the ball, both players moving in to net. In this fashion service is broken. And in a close match, a breakthrough takes immense pressure off the server whose delivery is coming up next.

XIII

Interminable Rallies and
How to End Them

The situation frequently arises where two players (the partner of each posted at net) exchange cross-court drives before one player loses the point through an error. Neither is able to take the net because of the accuracy and depth of the drives. If you are on one end of these exchanges and losing most of them because your opponent has more pace on the ball and is steadier, how do you make her miss? Ideally, you should wait for a short ball and take the net. But perhaps she seldom hits a short ball and you do not feel confident at the net anyway.

You must break up her rhythm of the exchange by using a variety of shots and searching for openings. You should return a drive with a sharp chop; with a floating ball that bounces high; with a shot hit with a great deal of top spin. You might lob over the opposing net player's head—and close in at net. Should your opponent return a short drive, you might try a sharply angled drop shot—again closing in at the net (she will be hitting up and you or your partner should be able to volley the ball away).

Since doubles is a two-player game, the net player

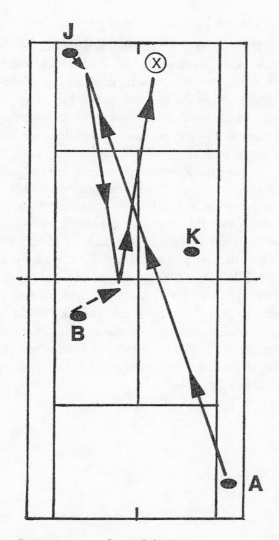

The Cutoff: During a prolonged forehand cross-court duel between Players A and J, rival Net Players B and K are both aware that they must put pressure on the opponent in backcourt and cut off the opponent's drive for the point. Net Player B, takes the risk of leaving her alley uncovered and quickly darts over to intercept J's drive to make the placement. If B knows that her Partner A loses most of these exchanges, she must play very boldly at net, putting enough pressure on J to make her hit a weak return or an error.

should enter into the duel; indeed, she should be the one who applies the pressure to force the implacable opponent to miss. She can poach, threaten to poach (see next chapter), leave an opening down her alley—tempting the opponent to hit there but quickly covering. She should be constantly on the move, carefully watching her partner's shots and those of the opponent, alert to the slightest chance to intercept the ball for a putaway. These maneuvers will disturb the opponent, perhaps forcing her to hit wide beyond the sideline; or to hit down the line, as a possible surprise maneuver, allowing the ball to be volleyed away for the point; or to miscalculate and hit a ball the net player can reach; or under pressure, to hit a weak lob that the net player can smash. It is reassuring to one's partner to have an alert, mobile player at net who is going to punish any mistake made by the opponent. In her zeal to upset the enemy, however, the net player should not leave her alley uncovered precipitately, for the return will surely zip down the vacated spot for a clean placement.

XIV

Pressuring the Opponents— the Poach

Doubles is a game of position (and of being caught out of position), but it is also a game of pressure. Pressure can cause loss of concentration, whittle away at one's confidence, and make a player hit a weak shot through tension. It can force an overambitious, flubbed shot or the netting of the easiest of putaways. Pressure is sometimes psychological: Getting mad at yourself for letting your side down, worrying because the opponents have spotted a chink in your side's armor; wondering in bewilderment how to halt your opponents' momentum.

But pressure is also tactical, and can be applied by tactical moves.

Pressure is caused by one team constantly taking the net and, if chased back, doggedly making the assault again. More pressure can be applied by vigilant use of the *poach*. Poaching—cutting across the net quickly to intercept an opponent's shot and putting it away—is a devastating weapon that should be made more use of by women players. It accomplishes the following: Ends a rally sharply and suddenly, helping to demoralize the opponents; forces opponents to hit wider, harder, and lower to keep the ball away from the poacher—causing errors to pile up; lures opponents to hit down the line (to keep the poacher honest) and being discomfited when the ball is casually angled for a placement; forces the opponents in their confusion to lob—limiting their offensive arsenal. One opponent in particular may be upset by her inability to keep the ball out of range of the peripatetic demon at the net and her stream of errors will make the difference between winning and losing the set.

Having an alert, aggressive poacher as a partner is very reassuring to the server. She knows that if she fires in a deep, well-placed serve, the return may be batted away for the point. There are few greater satisfactions for a doubles team; it is the zenith of co-operative effort. Should the receiver get the ball past the poacher, the latter is still a threat to any ground stroke that comes within three yards of her. All the server has to do is hit her drive deep cross court and the opposing team's next shot may go out of bounds. In addition, the poacher's constant movement intimidates the opponents, making them wonder where they can hit a safe shot, and if now is the time they are going to be outguessed.

Not every player can be a successful poacher. It requires certain physical and mental skills—the ability to volley well, anticipate an opponent's shot, and move fast laterally; and a willingness to take risks. (All these qualities can be improved, of course, in practice sessions and practice matches.) In a sense, the poacher is like a quarterback. She must determine, after several games, the pattern of each opponent's play—in addition to gauging what help she can receive from her own partner. She must have confidence in her decisions—whether to commit herself by tearing along the net before the return is hit (to cut off a widely angled cross-court shot), or to wait for the opponent to start her swing before making her move; or to pretend to poach and dart back to her original position. As the set unfolds, observations should be filed away. Is a serve to the deuce-court receiver's backhand usually hit slowly cross court? (Perhaps a few of these can be cut off.) Does a wide serve to the ad-court receiver's backhand automatically trigger a shot down the line? (If so, the alley must be covered—and a volley for the point is automatic.) Does the receiver hit a forehand chop? (If she does, the poacher has more time to get to the ball and in most cases it will be rising as it crosses the net.) If her partner fails to put in the first serve, is it feasible, or disastrous, to poach on the second? How are the percentages running? Is her partner capable of keeping the rally going until the poacher can be dead sure of a putaway? Or should she get in there first—at whatever risk—because there is a poacher on the opposing side who slams back her partner's slow drives.

The poacher usually stands about one yard inside the singles sideline and about eight feet from the net, though the position will vary depending on the severity of her partner's serve, the tendency of a particular receiver to lob, and the confidence the poacher has in her ability to move right or left and hit crisp volleys. She should stand with the weight on the balls of her feet, balance equally distributed on each leg, racket held vertically in front of her chin or neck. She should carefully watch the ball as it enters the receiver's court, observe the receiver move into position to hit, and watch the ball as it comes off the receiver's racket. When she moves to cut off the ball, she must look at it constantly and hold her racket firm as she strikes it. The ball is hit with the flat of the strings in a punching motion and directed to an open portion of the court; the conventional volley is deep down the middle. If she lunges toward the ball and misses because of the angle at which it is hit, she should assume the server will return it and scramble back toward her alley to guard that part of the court. During rallies she can move farther over toward the middle of the court and closer to the net, since the opponents will probably have a deeper shot to return. If one opponent constantly lobs the return of serve, the poacher should play back farther to make ready to smash.

It is an inflexible rule that when a poacher makes the split-second decision to go all out for and strike at a ball, she must put the ball away if she can lay her racket on it. If she makes a weak, stabbing return, it is almost certain that the opponents will win the point, for the poacher's team will have left many spots on their court open. If the receiving team is handling service so confidently that poaching is either a waste of time or a losing battle, retrenching is advisable. The poach should be attempted only when a great serve forces a weak return or when the point score allows it (40–0 and perhaps 40–15). There is nothing more discouraging for a hard-working server than to have her partner at net overreach herself and zealously make a string of errors by unsuccessful poaches.

The poacher's partner, once she discovers her teammate's success, should think about setting up shots that the poacher can put away—deep serves to the opponents' forehand and backhand and deep cross-court returns that force defensive shots. She should also be ready to race for shots wide of the poacher's reach and for lobs that go over the poacher's head. With a good poacher at net, the server should make sure to get her first serve in; poaching on the second serve is generally unsafe—partly because the receiver has every confidence that she can slam the ball past or through the poacher.

An adjunct to the poach is the fake poach—pretending to move quickly toward the center of the court by turning in that direction, taking a step and then quickly returning to the original position, ready to move to either side. As the receiver prepares to hit, she notices, through peripheral vision, that the net player has moved to cut off an expected return. She slyly changes the direction of her swing and hits down the line—only to have the poacher quickly move toward the alley and angle away the return. Quite often the receiver, in a quandary as to whether to hit cross court out of the poacher's reach or for the apparently open alley, will flub the shot. The move by the poacher must be made early enough so that the receiver sees her intention and also so that the poacher can return to her original position. To have thus baited a successful trap is immensely satisfying to the serving team. And the fake poach, of course, sets up the real one.

The poacher will inevitably lose a few points for her side but if she is diligent and a good volleyer she will win many more than she loses because of the threat she represents. Poaching is a skill that should be experimented with and developed as much as any other.

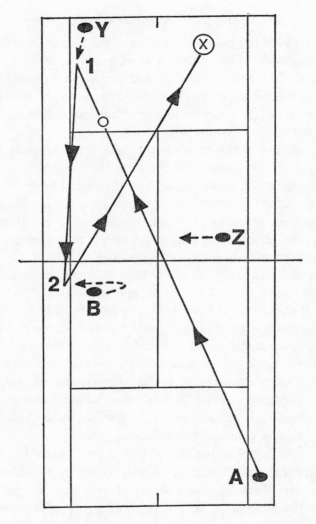

The Fake Poach: If carried out correctly, the poach frustrates a receiver because she is never sure if the net player is going to hold her ground or dart across to cut off the return. From a one-up-one-back formation, A has hit cross court to Y, who, seeing B head- and shoulder-fake to her right, anticipates a sure point if she hits down the line. B, having anticipated just such a supposition, switches direction as the ball is struck and pokes a placement between both opponents.

DEFENSE AGAINST THE POACH

What is a good defense when you are opposing a poacher? When receiving in the deuce court, if you can lob well, a safe tactic is to loft the ball over the poacher's head. It will not matter whether she has leapt to her right or not. The server has to take the ball on her backhand and your team can assume the offensive. From the ad court, lob diagonally to the server's backhand corner. The server may be able to take the ball on her forehand, but at least she is in the back of the court and the poacher has been frustrated. Another safe return, from either court, is the drop shot, which should be angled so sharply that there is no danger of its being intercepted. You can also keep the poacher reasonably honest by directing a drive down her alley from either service court (usually off the forehand in the deuce court, backhand in the ad court). Sharp-angled returns from either receiving court—they do not have to be hit hard—likewise are out of the poacher's reach. You may lose a few points while angling these shots but sooner or later you will perfect the timing.

It is useful to note where the poacher sends her volleys off both forehand and backhand. Down the middle? Toward your partner's feet? Angled toward the corners? All is not lost even if she makes a sound volley. Alert defenders can push the ball back several times and every return increases the chances of an error on the part of the attacking team.

During a rally, if you are far back and do not have confidence in the speed and placement of your drive, your

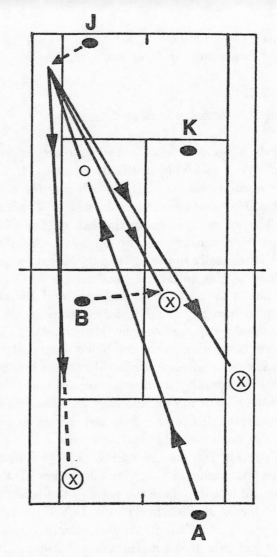

Defenses Against the Poacher: Player B, noted for her poaching, darts to her right to intercept a cross-court drive. Player J has her choice of: (1) lobbing over B's head, or (2) hitting a sharply angled cross-court drive beyond her reach, or (3) hitting a hard-to-handle low drive over the lowest part of the net. If B should move too soon in her poach, J, of course, will drive down the vacated alley. If the alley shot never comes, the net player can poach with impunity.

best tactic is to lob. However if you *do* have confidence in your drives, or if you hit from a point near the service line, you should angle the ball as far away from the poacher as possible within the bounds of safety, always alert to return a volley if the poacher should get her racket on your shot. You should also test her: Is her overhead strong? Is she as effective off the backhand side as the forehand? (Probably not.) Does she seem to have trouble with wildly spinning balls? Does she miss shots hit high to her backhand? If you find that, no matter what you and your partner do, the poacher manages to reach a large percentage of balls you send over the net you might, as a defensive measure, play back when your partner receives serve; your partner plays back when you receive serve. You are, in effect, forsaking the offensive, but sometimes prudence dictates such tactics because you will be better able to defend against the poaches—returning the majority of them with lobs.

The important thing while receiving serve or rallying, is not to pay more attention to the menace of the poacher than to the ball itself. If the poacher can keep you from concentrating on the ball she wins the struggle whether she makes spectacular shots or not.

XV

Right Court or Left?

Most doubles players have a definite preference as to which side of the court they play on, depending on their experience in that position and the kinds of shots they hit best. Some like to receive serve in the deuce court; other players are more at home on the other side. Some have absolutely no preference, adapting themselves to either side with ease. (Each player, of course, maintains that particular receiving position all through the set, after which sides can be switched, if desired.)

The specialties required are slightly different for the two positions. Generally the right-court player has an excellent forehand, good touch shots, and a sound tactical knowledge of the game (not that her partner doesn't). She should have a dependable return of serve, the ability to hit strongly cross court, a steady lob, and a strong forehand volley. She is equivalent to the setup man in volleyball and the playmaker in basketball.

The player who receives in the ad court should have a strong forehand that she can direct cross court to an opponent's backhand, a backhand she can depend on (since she will be taking a great many serves on that side), a more-than-adequate smash, an accurate lob off both sides, and the ability to volley well off both forehand and backhand. She should enjoy moving forward and powdering the ball. If either partner has good retrieving ability and is an expert at poaching, that is a definite plus.

Ideally, the deuce-court teammate keeps the ball in play and tries to force weak returns—ever aware that the opposing net player may put away any shot that ventures too close to her territory. The ad-court player does most of the smashing—like the spiker in volleyball—and takes almost everything that comes down the middle (lobs, drives, and volleys) on her forehand.

Out of habit, some players are uncomfortable playing a side they are not used to, but it is dangerous to overspecialize. In competition, strengths are rendered stronger but weaknesses are not given a chance to improve. During a game the right-court player often finds herself in the left court and vice versa. Lack of confidence in playing the unfamiliar side may result in the loss of points. In friendly doubles matches, players should switch sides every set or so to practice shots they ordinarily do not see much of: The confirmed deuce-court player, by switching, can practice receiving serves on her backhand and hitting forehands a little late so they will be directed to the opposing ad-court player's backhand. The confirmed ad-court player can practice sharply angled cross-court forehands and down-the-line lobs. In this way weaknesses can be corrected, new skills can be developed, and players can appreciate the difficulties that beset the partner who generally protects this particular side.

XVI

Duties of the Silent
(Non-stroking) Partner

The useful doubles teammate is always alert to the tactical aspects of a particular point even when the ball is not hit her way. If she is at net, she makes sure she looms as a threat; or she may tempt the opponents to hit to her by leaving a space on one side or the other which she is alert to cover. If the opponents move forward on a short ball, she stands in position ready to stretch for any hard drive that might be directed past her. If her partner has sent up a short lob, she moves back to the baseline to better cover her part of the court—expecting a smash. When her partner takes a short ball to hit a deep forcing shot, she moves up to the net parallel with her. (Sometimes on this shot she moves forward whether her partner is so inclined or not, hoping for a weak return and putting pressure on the opposing striker.)

When her partner is sent out of court to retrieve a wide shot, she quickly slips over to cover part of her partner's vacated side, ready to return a ball far to her right or far to her left and keep the rally going until her partner gets back into position. Though she has not hit the ball during a long exchange, she is always ready to enter the rally should the ball be hit her way—and is never caught off guard when it is. At net she covers her alley when an opening may be attacked but is not afraid to move away from it when she is sure the ball cannot safely be hit in that direction. She is constantly aware of the positioning of the opponents and the strengths, weaknesses, and tactical tendencies of each so that when she enters the rally she will know what shots to avoid and what shots give the greatest promise of putting the opponents in peril. If a ball comes down the middle that either she or her partner can hit, she moves into position to take it so that, if her partner backs off, the ball can be returned. If her partner, overambitious, moves out of position—even reaching for a ball and missing it, she is quick to move over and make the save if in a position to do so. She automatically crosses over to take lobs that sail over her partner's head—in plenty of time so that she will not hurry the shot.

Sometimes she eschews silence. In cases of lobs landing between her and her partner she is prompt to call out "Mine!" or "I've got it!"—"Yours!" or "Take it!" to mitigate any confusion. When her partner is about to hit a ball that is sailing out she calls "No!" or "Bounce it!" before the stroke is made. Sometimes, if she thinks her partner has not started forward soon enough to retrieve a wildly spinning ball she hollers "Up!" to galvanize her into action. If she sees that her lob is shallow and her partner is about to be murdered, she hollers "Back!" to save her partner's life.

If necessary, since both players are trying to win, she sometimes very tactfully gives her partner advice: "You have to watch her serve closely. She hits it right at the top of the toss and it's in your court before you know it."

Even tactics can be briefly discussed (though it is discourteous to discuss them too often): "Ellen loves to hit that down-the-line return when I serve to her forehand. Leave a little space to tempt her and move over as she hits." "Ethel is playing too close to the net. Lob over her head and we'll come up." "We're letting them take the net away from us. Let's keep our shots deep and get up there ourselves."

She encourages her partner by words, complimenting her on a placement or on a forcing shot that resulted in a return easily put away. And more by her *dependability* —at making steady returns difficult for the opponents to capitalize on, authoritatively demolishing sitters and showing by her quiet confidence that she is a member of a winning team.

XVII

If Your Partner Is Inexperienced

It often happens, as all are aware, that a fairly strong player may draw—in informal play or a club tournament or club match—a partner who is willing enough but who has taken up the game only recently, or is returning to it after a long layoff. Naturally, you face strong opposition.

This need not be the tragedy that seems to obtain at first glance. In singles, the weaker player is mercilessly exposed; in doubles this need not be the case. You, as the team's support, should note during the pre-contest rally where her strengths and weaknesses lie; or you may know from previous experience. If her forehand is her best stroke, she should play the right court; you can protect her backhand side if necessary. If her volleying is suspect, she should nonetheless play net on your serve—fairly close to it (about a yard away) and should stay close to the alley to prevent being passed with a down-the-line shot. It is up to you to do most of the retrieving.

If her return of serve is weak, giving the opposing net player many chances to control the ball, you should play about two yards in from the baseline—rather than close to the net—so that you will be better able to retrieve the net player's volleys. If your partner lobs short, quickly move back if you are at the net to cover some of the area into which the smash may be hit.

If you see that things are going badly because the opponents are taking advantage of your partner's weaknesses, you must take chances and keep the rallies short. The longer they go on, the more opportunities the opponents have to feed shots to your partner that she will miss. Your errors will mount up as you hit harder and try to come closer to the lines of course, but it is a tactic you should try. If the ad-court receiver is hammering your partner's backhand when she serves you might make use of the reverse serve formation for that court.

Before you serve you might suggest tactfully that your partner stay close to the alley to protect it. (Occasionally she will hit shots for placements.) Your first serve should go in about 75 per cent of the time; your second serve, in this situation, should be hit almost as hard as the first, even at the risk of occasional double faults. A hard second serve may take the receiver by surprise and score occasional points outright. A slow second serve, conversely, will be pounced on. The receiver may slam it back at your partner or pull you so far out of court that you leave a large opening into which the opponents can hit.

While you are spreading yourself thin all over the court, you should be watching for possible weaknesses in both your opponents. Test them with lobs, drop shots, drives hit directly at the net player, excessive spin, nervousness when you climb all over the net. Maybe one of them is slow afoot, lacks a backhand, or has no sense of where she should position herself during rallies. These weaknesses should be ferreted out and taken advantage of as the opportunity arises.

And beyond this, you must be a psychoanalyst. You

should retain a cheery outlook no matter how bad things look for your side. (It is important in this situation not to fall behind if you can help it. Let us say you have lost the first set while analyzing the opposition and making adjustments. Start the next set off with a bang so as not to have to play come-from-behind tennis.) Do not pout if your partner misses easy shots and give her encouragement when she makes a good return that the opponents miss.

Even if your side loses the point but your partner has played good tennis, acknowledge it. If you should happen to miss a shot, do not overreact, as this may upset your partner, who is probably well aware of her own shortcomings and the fact that she's not being much help to you. Do not burden her with more pressure than she already feels.

XVIII

Playing with a
Left-handed Partner

A left-handed doubles partner is good news. When your team is receiving she would ordinarily play on the left, you the right. Here you have both wings strong; power off both sides, enabling you to rake the opponents' court with cross-court forehands.

More good news: A left-hander's serve is often troublesome to the receiver, since it comes at her at a different angle, and the spin of the ball after it hits the floor is different from what she is accustomed to. This means occasional outright errors but mainly weak returns that you, at net, can pounce on for quick points. Great pressure is put on the receiver—especially in the ad court. The serve naturally curves over to the receiver's backhand and the middle of the opponents' court should be open for a putaway volley or smash.

When your lefty partner plays net she is troublesome for the opponents because she will be poaching mainly in the ad court—her forehand covering vast expanses to her left. If you can serve to the receiver's backhand (the classic spot), your side should glean many points by her net play. In the deuce court, playing farther to the right than a right-handed player, she will score many points on the receiver's down-the-line shots directed (surprise!) at her forehand. A lob that goes over her left shoulder (the safest place to lob for righties) will be smashed down hard.

All these successes will undoubtedly be disconcerting to the opponents, who will probably have to ruminate before each shot: Where is she? Where is the strength distributed? How much territory can she cover with that incalculable reach of hers?

The middle, of course, will be your weakness, covered by two backhands. But you know the opponents are going to aim there when your side is at net and you can be ready for them. Conventionally, on a ball down the middle, the player who hit the last shot moves in and makes the volley. However, if your partner's backhand is weak, you should take the ball; if yours is weak she should take it. But your play should be so aggressive and demoralizing that the opponents will not be able to aim accurately much of the time and you can take many of these shots on your forehands.

In case of a lob down the middle, the player with the stronger overhead should move over to take it (no excuse for not taking this because it's your backhand) after giving proper warning: "I got it!" or "Mine!"

ADVICE TO THE LEFT-HANDER (should she need it)

Being left-handed is an immense advantage in most sports, especially tennis. Right-handers are not used to the spin on your shots and it is inevitable that your strongest shot—a cross-court drive—attacks their weakest side. Most of the time, opponents will automatically hit to your strength (being programmed by years of play to attack the left side) and be surprised by the power and accuracy of your return. The conventional serve in the ad court—to the backhand—turns up on your forehand, where you can sweep the ball cross court and follow it to net. When you are at net, what should be your weak side turns out to be the strong one.

Tactically, you should play very aggressive doubles, aware that your opponents will be confused for a while, at least. Your partner should play aggressively, too, moving in at every opportunity. Should you miss a few shots, forget it; the percentages are all with you.

OPPOSING A LEFTY-RIGHTY COMBINATION

Faced with this problem, what recourse do right-handers have?

In the first place, they should remember at all times that they are playing against a left-hander and that conventional tactics go out the window. Nearly every shot—volley, drive, lob—should be aimed down the middle, to the backhands (most of the time) of the two opponents. Even when their forehands are covering the middle, the placement may confuse them.

Serves to the ad court should be directed to the lefty's backhand; even if she manages to take them on her forehand she will not have the sharp angle that she would have otherwise. Once in a while serve flat to the left side of the service box. If she is far away, you may score an ace.

With the left-hander at net and the serve coming to your side's deuce court, the receiver should hit drives cross court or lob over the lefty's head; a down-the-line shot is suicidal. In the ad court, however, if the receiver has a good down-the-line backhand, she can crack the ball to the lefty's backhand and may be rewarded with a point or weak reply. (A *forehand* down-the-line shot off the serve in the ad court can be risky.) Cross-court returns from the ad court must be angled sharply to avoid a poach. If the lefty continually poaches successfully—on serve returns or during rallies—the striker's partner should play close to the baseline instead of near the net to help defend the territory into which the lefty is volleying.

If the lefty consistently wins points by returning serve to the server's undependable backhand, the Australian or reverse serve formation should be resorted to. (See next chapter.)

Should she follow her serve to net: From the deuce court, hit a hard cross-court return or a soft, low-bouncing return that she will have to scoop up on her backhand; or lob over the net player's head. From the ad court, lob over the net player's head, hit a hard forehand drive down the middle of the court or a hard cross-court forehand. If the serve is a deep, spinning one to the backhand, your safest return is a lob hit to the middle of the court or a deep cross-court lob.

XIX

The Reverse Serve
(Australian) Formation

Sometimes for tactical or psychological reasons a doubles team wishes to assume the reverse serve formation. This calls for the net player to position herself on the same side of the court as the server. It is used most often when the server serves to the ad court, particularly against a receiver who has a powerful cross-court shot which would be attacking the server's backhand. (A receiver who is able to take most of the shots on her forehand, for instance; or a player with a strong backhand; or, in particular, a left-hander with a strong cross-court drive.)

With the server's partner stationed at the net, about a yard away from the center service line and a yard or so behind the net (instead of in or near the alley), this forceful cross-court shot is taken away from the ad-court receiver. The server takes her position very close to the center service mark, anticipating a quick run to her right to hit back a possible down-the-line return from the receiver.

When the server serves to the deuce court, if the formation is used, the net player stands in the right-hand side of the court, about a yard or so from the net and about a yard from the center service line.

The formation is useful (1) when the server is weak off one side and the receivers know they can successfully attack it; (2) when one receiver or the other has a very tricky drop shot that catches the server back in the court. This reverse formation also confuses the opponents because it is unorthodox.

The formation has a number of weaknesses, however. The receiver in the deuce court can hit down the line and make the server hustle over to her left to make the retrieve; she can lob cross court over the net player's head, making the receiver hustle to her right; she can slam the ball at the net player, who may make a weak volley; she can hit a down-the-line drop shot (admittedly a difficult stroke), which may cause both members of the serving team to ponder a moment before one of them charges for it, very likely making a weak return.

In the ad court, the same options hold: The receiver can hit down the line, lob over the net player's head, slam the ball at the net player, or hit a down-the-line drop shot.

A great burden is placed on the net player in this formation, particularly if she is not accustomed to it. But, if the tactics demand it, she must station herself on the same side of the court as the server—sort of like a linebacker shifting over to plug a hole in the line. She must be quite agile and anticipate well, since the receivers will test her ability to cover her increased share of the court and whip drives to both sides of her. She must be fast on her feet, for she will be called on to scoop up occasional drop shots. And she should be ready to back up to take cross-court lobs, taking some of the burden off the server.

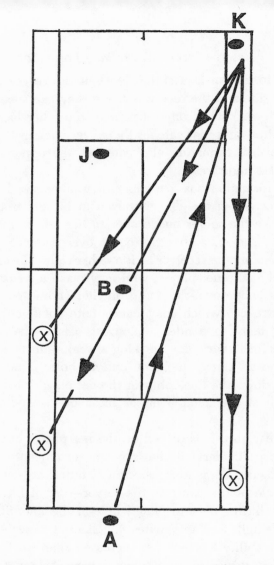

Defenses Against the Australian Formation: With Net Player
B standing in Partner A's half of the court (presumably to
protect A's uncertain backhand), Receiver K has two attacking serve returns: A backhand drive down the line which will
force Server A to sprint to her right; and a lob lofted over B's
head into A's backhand corner. A third possible return is a
sharply angled cross-court shot behind B, should she be
moving forward and to her right.

The server, too, must be speedy, for at various times she will be racing to her right, to her left and toward the net. The formation is not recommended against a heady receiving team, since one or both members of the serving team will have to labor like a slave in a quarry to keep from losing the game.

DEFENSE AGAINST THE REVERSE FORMATION

The best return for the deuce-court receiver is a drive down the alley, making the server dash over to hit it back with her backhand. If the serve comes short to the receiver's forehand, she can angle the ball between the server and the net player. A cross-court lob is another favored return, since it allows the receiving team to take the net.

In the ad court the receiver has a similar choice of shots, down the line being preferred. A shallow serve to the backhand can be directed between the server and net player, while a lob to the server's backhand puts the serving team on the defensive.

XX

Sure Cure for Ragged Play—Doubles

Because of the nature of the game—pressure applied, mistakes quickly punished—inexplicable slumps occur more often in doubles than in singles. You may find at some point in the set that every return of serve you hit either flies into the net or is easily reachable by the opposing net player; that the opponents keep hitting to you during rallies, confident that you will eventually miss (you don't disappoint them); that you are blowing sitters at net you should put away wearing a sleeping mask; that your second serve threatens your partner with evisceration. Your partner encourages you (though you suspect what she is thinking) and you become increasingly tense. You feel you are letting your partner down and you have two more witnesses to your ignominy.

As in singles, you must restore concentration and, with that, confidence in your shots. The ball is supposed to go where you aim it. As in singles, thrust your entire concentration at the ball, forgetting your partner's discouragement, enemy attacks, and your own backlog of errors. Hitting down the middle gives you the safest margin, so aim shots there for a while. If pressed, send up a high lob. Make sure your first serve goes in. Assume that every shot your opponents hit is going to be aimed your way, whether you are at net or in the back of the court. Do not hurry when changing courts or picking up balls or making ready to serve; allow tension to subside.

From a psychological standpoint, reassure your partner. This will make her feel better about the valiant efforts she has been making to keep your side in the ball game and will remove some of the pressure that has been tightening up your forearm muscles. Don't alibi and don't act discouraged; the effects of a losing psychology can be contagious. Think positively.

XXI

Mixed Doubles

The days are long gone when a male player would suggest to his female partner, "Hie yourself to the net, honey, close to the sideline, and don't leave that spot. I'll handle everything else that lands on this side of the net."

Today, women tennists have immensely improved in the severity of their strokes, ability to cover court, and knowledge of what to do with the ball. As women's tennis costumes have undergone a revolution, so has their expertise in the game itself. They no longer giggle when they miss but resolve to hit the next shot harder and with more precision. It is no longer considered unladylike or unrefined to run or breathe hard or slam a tennis ball— even at a male opponent.

Much more is expected of women tennis players today, and they are happy to oblige. Women are often asked to make a fourth when three men are arranging a game and most of them have no trouble holding their own. They are not deterred by a male player when a fourth is needed by three women. As an adjunct to this, they have responded nobly to the national physical fitness drive— jogging, swimming, and doing calisthenics (not always motivated by improving their tennis, of course)—and the result is they are often in better condition than many of the males they play with.

Mixed doubles is usually played more for fun than for blood, but you may find it useful to consider the special tactics involved. (We are assuming, for the sake of challenge, that the male partner and the male opponent play strong games—experienced, fast, and keenly competitive.)

TACTICS AND LA DIFFÉRENCE

The difference between facing a good male opponent and a good woman opponent across the net in doubles is usually this: The man's serve is harder and generally carries more spin. He can generally place it better. His second serve, while slower, will carry even more spin. The woman receiver must accept a good many serves on her backhand in the deuce court because by playing too far to the left she may be aced. Wide to the forehand is a favorite shot of many deuce-court men servers when delivering to women. His forehand is usually hit quite hard; sometimes with considerable top spin which causes the ball to take a long, high bounce. His backhand can vary from fair to excellent. He has probably perfected a greater variety of shots than you are accustomed to in women's doubles: Chop, various kinds of cuts, disguised drop shot, reliable half volley. He may take the ball on the rise on his forehand and backhand preparatory to coming to net. He may serve an American Twist and come to net behind it. Most men like to play net in doubles and are reasonably good retrievers.

The tactics indicated by this situation, assuming your partner is of nearly equal ability to his counterpart across the net, is to keep the ball away from the male opponent as much as possible and direct your attack at the woman player; as indeed the opposition will be directing theirs toward you.

The Serve

(If you are certain the male player has a better serve than you, ignore his sense of chivalry and insist that he serve first. He will serve more often than you, or at least as often, during the set and this may result in a swing of several games. On the other hand, if his serve is so-so but he is good at the net, you should serve first.)

You should try hard when serving to place most deliveries on the receiver's backhand. This may force the woman receiver to hit a weak return which your partner can put away at the net. If the ball is to her forehand she will surely keep it out of the net player's reach. The male receiver, in the ad court, will probably not be as strong on the backhand side. Again, his weak return of a deep serve may be angled away for a placement by the net player. Because of your partner's imposing presence at the net and the possibility of his making a successful poach against the woman receiver, you should make sure to get the first serve in. (It is extremely unwise to double-fault to the woman opponent. If you are going to double-fault, restrict it to the ad court.) Getting the first serve in is important in the ad court, too, if your second serve is weak. A weak serve gives the receiver a chance to slam the ball directly at your partner at net; or to hit deep to your backhand, following the shot to net; or to hit a drop shot to your backhand that you will have difficulty in reaching.

If the woman opponent hits a deep cross-court return, you should drive cross court back to her unless she has come to the net. In that case, your safest shot is a cross-court lob. Other alternatives: If the male player is far to his right, with a view to cutting off your drive, you can hit down the line or lob over his head. (Neither of these shots is as safe as the first two, but it is important to make the pattern of your returns flexible and to keep the opponents guessing.)

If the return from the deuce court is shallow, move in on it and hit down the middle to the woman player's backhand or sharply cross court. Or hit a cross-court drop, bringing her in. In the event that the serve return from either court is a lob to your backhand, hit a drive to the woman opponent if she is back, making sure the shot is deep. If she has come to net, the safest return is a high lob directed to her portion of the court. (Some male players invade this territory to smash the lob.)

Your opponents will have figured, as will have your team, that breaking the serve of the woman player on the opposite side is the surest way to pick up enough games for the set. Thus your serve will be carefully exploited and you must be sure not to give away easy points, or be pressured by a constantly moving net player into making an error through loss of concentration. Try especially hard to win the deuce-court point, as you will then have a lead when serving to the ad court—and the pressure may cause the receiver to overextend himself.

Return of Serve

The woman partner conventionally receives in the

deuce court, where she can receive service with her forehand. This allows the male player to take shots down the center on his forehand. He is also in position to smash lobs that come down the center and anywhere to his left. Presumably he has a reasonably strong backhand, so the extreme left of the court is protected and he can hit deep cross-court shots with it.

If the serve comes to your forehand—the woman opponent serving—your safest return is a cross-court drive to her forehand. Your partner will probably move up to net, ready to cut off the return. If your shot is deep, you should move in with him—but be ready to retreat for a lob. If the serve is to your backhand, again you should hit cross court. Other returns off forehand and backhand are lobs over the net player's head and cross-court drop shots. If the woman server comes to net behind her serve, the best return is a low drive that will land at about her feet, forcing her to hit up, or a lob over her head. If the net player keeps poaching or threatening to poach, hit a drive down his alley. You should attack a weak second serve and come behind it to net—the volley made by you or your partner is perhaps the surest way of winning the point.

Should you be receiving in the ad court, you should play far to the left on the woman opponent's serve if your forehand is much the stronger stroke, and drive deep to her backhand, following the shot to net. A cross-court drop shot is very effective on this side. If pulled out of court on the left by a serve to the backhand, your best recourse is a deep cross-court lob. If you have confidence in your backhand, you might in this circumstance hit down the line to catch the net player napping—though if he is not, you have lost the point for your side.

When the male opponent serves, you must be prepared for slightly more speed and spin. You must move into position and get your racket back more quickly to meet the ball. The spin off the slice serve will cause the ball to bounce slightly to the right and your return will tend to go to the right—where the net player can reach it if you do not hit solidly.

You can drive cross court or lob—the important thing is to return the ball, putting the burden of winning the point on the serving team. If the net player leaves her alley uncovered, shoot a drive down her backhand side; her riposte may be weak. If the male server runs up to net, your best returns are a low, hard drive or a low, shallow drive that he may have trouble volleying, or a lob over the net player's head. If the last is your constant reply, the server will stop running to net because he merely has to run back to the baseline again.

In serving the American Twist, which some male players do, the back is markedly arched and the racket is brought across the top and left side of the ball, imparting severe top spin and right-to-left sidespin. The bounce is to the left of the receiver and after being hit the ball tends to travel to the left—precisely opposite from the slice serve. Your best recourse for this serve is to swing solidly through the ball, concentrating on a smoothly hit cross-court return, your aim point being about two feet over the middle of the net. If you lob, aim for the center of the court so that the ball will not sail beyond the sidelines.

Rallying

The same principles apply as to rallying in women's doubles: Keep the ball deep, lob when in trouble, keep the ball away from the net player, mix up your shots so that the opponent cannot groove his or her swing, concentrate on meeting the ball.

In rallying with the woman player you should make every effort to close in at net, since her male partner is waiting to cut off a drive that veers wide or one hit without sufficient speed. In fact, he may go hunting for it. (Your partner will of course be doing the same thing. But merely your act of going forward to press the issue may cause your rival to hit a weak shot.) If you go to net, the chances are that the reply will be hit to you, so be ready to volley to an open point in the other side's court. If a lob is sent up as you go in, your partner may be in position to smash it. If he is not, halt, drop back, and smash down the middle, preferably to the woman opponent's backhand.

The male player, when you exchange shots with him, will probably try to overwhelm you with speed or, if that doesn't work, with spins or a chop. You must watch his stroke carefully to see how he draws his strings across the ball—under it (chop) or sidewise, imparting slice. Slice put on the backhand causes the ball to bounce to your right, away from your forehand; slice on the forehand causes the ball to bounce to your left, away from your backhand. You don't necessarily have to remember which way the ball will bounce; just be aware that it must be watched carefully after bouncing and the spin must be removed by hitting solidly through it. A chop, of course, floats to some extent and its bounce is more vertical than that of a drive. The return must be aimed slightly higher than that of a drive or the ball will land short in the opponent's court or in the net.

If you are confronted with a drive carrying a great deal of top spin, you should take it back a little farther and wait till it descends to waist height before hitting it. The alternative is to return it from about shoulder height with a chop on either forehand or backhand.

If you find you are being overpowered or outcutted in your rallies with the male opponent, you have several choices: Get up to net, where his variety of spins will not make much difference; lob over the net player's head to drive her back, after which your team's attack can be directed her way; hit a hard drive at or past the net player, which may win a point or inspire a weak return. You can also make arrangements with your partner at net to poach when, for instance, the ball is hit by the opponent the second time during a rally. It may confuse the opposition.

Should you be confronted by both opponents at the net, your safest shot is a lob down the middle or over the woman player's head. Next is a low soft drive down the middle that will have to be hit up by one of the opponents. Finally, a flat-out low passing shot to an opening on one side or the other. During play you should experiment with each type of return to see which is the most effective and against whom. Remember: Give your opponents every chance to miss.

Net Play

When your partner serves to the woman opponent you

should be on the alert for a weak return that you can put away—the situation is one that should earn your team a great many points. If the serve is hard, carries spin, and is well placed, the receiver will not be able to place it where she wishes. She may send up a shallow lob that you can smash or a soft drive that you can volley away for the point.

You should not be content with merely returning the ball but hit it solidly and hard to an opening. Failing to make a point off a weak shot is almost as bad as making an error off it. After you have put away a few of your opponent's returns, the pressure on her will be considerable and her confidence may dissipate on less difficult shots.

The male receiver will presumably handle the serve with more ease but again you should be ready to volley away a weak return. On wide serves to his backhand, make sure you cover the alley to guard against the tempting down-the-line shot. If you are in position, you have a sure point with a volley hit deep to the middle of the court.

In rallies, you should keep watching for a chance to cut off a drive by one or the other of your opponents, moving to the right or left along the net as the bounce point of your partner's shot dictates and noting open spots on the opponents' court into which a volley can be sent. Sometimes faking a poach during a rally will upset the striker enough so that he or she hits a weak shot or errs—especially if you have scored a number of successes with your volleys.

On deep shots hit by your partner, especially if he has come to net, expect a lob return and quickly make the decision as to who should take it. Generally your partner will shout "Mine!" or "Yours!" to halt any confusion.

If your partner, in trouble, lofts a lob that you can see is going to land shallow, scurry back to the baseline to cover part of the court—and be alert to retrieve a soft shot near the net as an alternative to a hard smash.

If you are in a close-range volleying and half-volleying duel with one or both opponents at net, try to hit low, soft shots that force the striker to hit up. If you manage this, move in on the ball and hit down on it—the direction does not much matter, as long as your shot lands in the court.

When both you and your partner are at net, you can expect to be the target of most of the shots. Your purpose in aiming your volleys should be to open up the middle by hitting to the sides or opening up the sides by hitting to the middle. You should not take more than three volleys to win a point, however, since your chances of error or being passed increase with each shot.

A woman partner who plays net well and likes to play net is a great source of support and joy to her partner. Two players at net are three and a half times as effective as one, and if the male player makes a good forcing shot he likes to see it put away, he doesn't care by whom.

ADDENDUM

Not all male players are as skilled as those hypothesized above. Some have no backhands, some are leery of the net, and some have injuries that slow them down. If you should get one as a partner, review the paragraphs in the Women's Doubles section on playing with an inexperienced partner, changing "her" to "him." If your woman opponent gets one, go easy on him. It's only a game.

Whether the game is played for the exercise it provides, as a novelty, or something to be carefully tabulated in one's record book, mixed doubles should be approached in a spirit of great good will. If the sides are markedly unequal, the good players should hit easy shots to the poor ones and rallies should not be terminated with one blast. Courtesies should be extended liberally to the opponents, the score should not be argued about lengthily, and the tactical errors of one's partner should be excused. Women players will receive compliments from their partner and from their opponents which should be volleyed back. The test of a good match is whether all the players enjoyed themselves, with the notation that winners enjoy themselves more than losers.

XXII

The Elements

Tennis is not always played under ideal conditions. Sometimes it is hot and sometimes it is chilly. Dress warmly, at least while warming up, for the latter, and carefully pace yourself for the former. Wind is another matter. It directly affects the speed and direction of the ball and can be an insidious enemy or a beneficent friend, depending on how you use it. Unless you are playing in a gale, it should not disturb you unduly.

When you step onto the court, notice if there is a wind and, if so, in which direction it is blowing, how strong it is, and whether or not it comes in gusts. A flag on a pole will sometimes indicate this (though for a height much greater than that of the court surface), but a handkerchief loosely held is better. Or you can toss up a handful of grass, as golfers do.

While warming up you can further gauge the speed, direction, and eccentricities of the wind. Having it behind you adds speed to your shots and removes speed from your opponent's. There is a psychological factor, too. In a sense your opponent is battling the elements—wind in her face, her drives slowed down, her lobs hindered in their forward flight, while all you have to do is flick the ball and it sails right over the net.

You should take immediate advantage of the situation,

coming to net behind drives and taking advantage of short shots that will inevitably be hit by your opponent. Her drives when you are at net will approach you more slowly than usual, giving you plenty of time to put them away. Her lobs will be held up by the wind. They may be difficult to judge while descending, but after they bounce (more toward the vertical than usual) you will often have an easy smash for the point. Your first serve will come in harder—though if you find it consistently goes out, you should aim lower, perhaps making a correction in your toss.

Chopped strokes are likely to carry beyond the base-line; imparting top spin is safer, while flat drives should not be hit as hard as usual. Keep a sharp watch to see if the wind is gusty or changing direction—staying loyal or defecting, as it were.

It is very important to win games when you have the wind behind your back; on the change of courts the advantage will be with your opponent.

With the wind against you, your opponent will be on the attack. You must hit your drives harder and deeper than usual to avoid giving her short shots that she can come in on. Chopped drives, making the ball rise nearly vertically after the bounce, may draw some errors. When you lob, make sure the lob goes deep enough. If your opponent is giving you fits by driving deep and taking the net, try to get up there first yourself. Maybe she will start hitting drives or lobs beyond the baseline in her efforts to dislodge you.

If the wind is blowing from your left to your right, you can hit hard to your opponent's forehand, but you must be careful how wide you hit to her backhand. Down-the-line forehand drives are dangerous because the wind may take them out. At net in singles you should play slightly to the right of where you would ordinarily play. A shot to your left will be brought closer, while one you cannot reach on your right may veer past the sidelines. In doubles, when the serve is to the deuce court you can move farther away from the alley than usual—but watch for a shot down there, because your opponent knows the wind will keep the ball in. In the ad court, play your usual position—but you may find you can reach a cross-court return more readily because the wind will be pushing it in your direction.

When the wind comes from right to left, shots should be hit to the opponent's backhand; cross-court forehands should not be angled too wide or they may be carried out. At net in singles you can play farther to the left. In doubles, when at net in the deuce court, play your usual position; a drive down the alley that you cannot reach will sail out. You should figure on intercepting some cross-court drives that will be wafted toward you. When the serve is to the ad court, watch out for a down-the-line shot.

The threat of the poacher is magnified in a windy situation. In their efforts to avoid her, opponents may find their shots carried past the sidelines.

In serving, you can score occasional aces by placing the ball wide in the service box, the wind adding speed and making spin more effective. You should, however, try to get the vast majority of first serves in, since chances of a double fault are much greater on a windy day. If you are having trouble with your toss drifting, make the toss lower and hit the serve a little bit sooner.

In smashing, you will probably make errors if you hit the ball before it bounces. Let it bounce and then, judging its height and downward movement precisely, make sure of your shot.

In doubles, always be aware of the wind direction and force so that an opponent's shot down the middle is automatically taken care of by you or your partner without wasting time on deliberation.

The sun likewise affects tactics. Lobs that force the net player to look into it draw errors or soft returns that can be easily handled, sometimes even put away. If the opponents face the sun they should be lobbed frequently while at net and their tentative returns pounced on. An additional factor is that the smasher, having glanced at the sun momentarily, may find her vision impaired for a second or two. She may therefore be unable to handle a brisk riposte.

If you are looking into the sun and confronted with a lob, you are probably better off letting the ball bounce and drop to hip height, and then hit out with a drive or sharp chop.

If the sun is in the server's eyes, it is likely that her serve will not be very severe; she will be more interested in getting it into the court. In doubles, it should be returned to her part of the court, since she may be temporarily blinded by looking at the sun during the toss. (Do you want to be kind or be a winner?)

To keep from looking at the sun, the server has two courses of action. She can move back and forth on the baseline until she finds a spot where the sun provides the least glaring light. Or she can toss the ball to the side and low, waiting till it comes to about six inches above the right shoulder and hit it with her elbow sharply bent to impart pronounced slice. This serve, easy to control, spins over the net without much clearance and the bounce is low because of the sidespin imparted. The server does not have to look in the sun at all. It is a most useful serve under these circumstances and should be practiced if it is felt the sun is going to cause trouble.

In doubles, if you have a left-handed partner, check to see if she can serve facing the sun with less difficulty than you, the right-hander. If both players are right-handed, the weaker server should serve into the sun, if she can be persuaded to. In mixed doubles, the man should be the hero. Needless to say, it is vital to get the first serve in (except in the case of the sharply sliced serve mentioned above). Otherwise the server has two looks at the sun instead of one.

COURT SURFACES

The type of court surface and occasionally the condition of the court markedly affect play. Some shots are more effective on one surface than another and thus tactics vary. Most players greatly favor one type of surface over another.

Surfaces can be roughly classified into fast, slow, and halfway between. The fast surfaces—furnishing a low bounce, with the ball often skidding as it hits—require that the player hit the ball fairly close to the ground. They include grass, wood (as in armories), and cement. The racket must be drawn back very fast and care must be taken not to hit too late, for the ball shoots up like a rocket after it bounces.

Slow surfaces—furnishing a high bounce, the ball, comparatively speaking, hanging in place and waiting to be hit—include clay and some composition courts. More time can be taken with the shot.

Surfaces midway between the two include asphalt and some of the new composition courts. The bounce of the ball is not as slow as on clay but a good deal slower than on grass or cement.

Wet grass and wet clay slow down the ball a great deal—indeed, on wet grass the ball hardly bounces at all.

Fast courts are favored by serve-and-volley players. A hard shot that lands in the opponent's court is very difficult to place accurately, and players take advantage of this by taking the net. The latter maneuver also means they will not have to contend with the ricochet bounce. Rallies are generally short and the server has a distinct advantage. Hard serves, flat drives, smashes, and sharp volleys are most effective on fast courts.

Slow courts are favored by good retrievers, baseline players, and thinkers rather than extremely hard hitters. Speed is taken off the ball after it bounces, and volleys, angled shots, and smashes that would be placements on the faster surface can be rescued on clay. Ability to keep the ball in play and outmaneuvering the opponent are the skills that win points.

If a court has an extremely low bounce or if there are

holes in the surface, it is a good idea to get to net and avoid the problems occasioned by these factors.

Indoor courts (except for wood) are usually slow, with good retrieves frequent and rallies long. On many indoor courts you cannot rely on the lob so much because it will hit a girder or the ceiling or light fixture, awarding the point to the opponents. If the lob is kept low, it is likely to be smashed by the opposition. Passing shots and soft, low drives are used much more in indoor play. You may also find, when first playing indoors, because of the unusual perspective, that you hit many balls short or into the net; the serve also lands into the net. In serving, if this is the case, aim for the baseline rather than the rear service line; in hitting drives aim several feet over the net.

With the co-operation of the United States Lawn Tennis Association, Doubleday has published the following titles in this series:

SPEED, STRENGTH, AND STAMINA: Conditioning for Tennis, by Connie Haynes with Eve Kraft and John Conroy.
Detailed descriptions of exercises for tennis players, and suggestions for keeping in shape.

TACTICS IN WOMEN'S SINGLES, DOUBLES, AND MIXED DOUBLES, by Rex Lardner.
A book for women tennis players, with specific suggestions for taking advantage of opponents' weaknesses.

SINISTER TENNIS, by Peter Schwed.
How to play against left-handers and with left-handers as doubles partners.

The following titles are in preparation:

FINDING AND EXPLOITING YOUR OPPONENT'S WEAKNESSES

RETURN OF SERVICE

COVERING THE COURT

GROUND STROKES

SPECIALIZATION IN SINGLES, DOUBLES, AND MIXED DOUBLES

THE SERVE AND THE OVERHEAD

THE HALF VOLLEY AND THE VOLLEY

TEACHING TENNIS

TENNIS AS A THERAPY

SKILLS AND DRILLS

Each book in this series is illustrated with line drawings and is available in both hardcover and paperback editions.